Paula Rinehart unmasks the myth that nonmarital sex is harmless. She carefully undresses a woman's pain to reveal the scarred soul that lies beneath the illusion that sexual intimacy is merely a physical act. But she doesn't leave bare this reality. She redresses it by sensitively detailing God's intent for married sex. A woman who wants to experience spiritual and emotional wholeness is gently led back to the path of purity to walk in the freedom ushered in by God-esteem, dignity, and self-respect.

LAVERNE TOLBERT, author of *Keeping Your Kids Sexually Pure*

Praise for *Sex and the Soul of a Woman*

In our sex-crazed society, *Sex and the Soul of a Woman* elevates both sex and womanhood. Paula Rinehart gives hope and healing and shows practically how to internalize boundaries. We highly recommend this spiritually thought-provoking book.

LINDA DILLOW AND LORRAINE PINTUS,
authors of *Intimate Issues* and *Gift-Wrapped by God*

Finally, a fresh, modern book that allows a woman to fully understand the impact of a sexual relationship. If we could have learned earlier the worth we bring to men instead of the shame we often bring into our lives, many of our wounds could have been avoided. If I could pick one book for every woman I know to read, regardless of her background, it would be *Sex and the Soul of a Woman*.

JAMIE, Grand Rapids, Michigan

I saw myself throughout the pages of this book—big-time! It helped for someone to validate my feelings of regret and loss during the time of my life that included one relationship after another with men. It's the book I wish someone had put in my hands then.

FRAN, Costa Mesa, California

So many of us know that sexual intimacy outside of marriage is a cheapened form, at best. What we often don't know is the most freeing and life-giving part—the why. This book offers hope and meaning in an arena where we sometimes doubt the goodness of God. Never before has my sexual dependence on God struck me so hard. Without him, all I have to offer a man is an act.

STEPHANIE, Washington, D.C.

It was refreshing for me to be affirmed in the value of sexual innocence. I'm comforted to realize that God has placed boundaries around sexuality because of our tremendous importance to him.

CAROLYN, Calgary, Alberta, Canada

I'm a well-educated twenty-two-year-old woman, and this is the first time I've heard some of the ideas put forth in this book. It helped me most by making me think about "God being inside sex." The whole book made me think about romance and sex differently.

JENA, Roanoke, Virginia

Sex and the Soul of a Woman

How God Restores the
Beauty of Relationship
from the Pain of Regret

Paula Rinehart

ZONDERVAN®

ZONDERVAN.com/
AUTHORTRACKER
follow your favorite authors

ZONDERVAN

Sex and the Soul of a Woman
Copyright © 2004, 2010 by Paula Rinehart

Requests for information should be addressed to:

Zondervan, *Grand Rapids, Michigan 49530*

Library of Congress Cataloging-in-Publication Data

Rinehart, Paula.
    Sex and the soul of a woman : how God restores the beauty of relationship
from the pain of regret / Paula Rinehart.
        p.   cm.
    Includes bibliographical references.
    ISBN 978-0-310-32989-3 (softcover)
    1. Sex—Religious aspects—Christianity. 2. Christian women—Religious life.
I. Title.
BT708.R49 2010
241'.66—dc22   2010028023

Any Internet addresses (websites, blogs, etc.) and telephone numbers printed in this
book are offered as a resource. They are not intended in any way to be or imply an
endorsement by Zondervan, nor does Zondervan vouch for the content of these sites
and numbers for the life of this book.

Published in association with the literary agency of Alive Communications, Inc., 7680
Goddard Street, Suite 200, Colorado Springs, CO 80920. www.alivecommunications
.com

Cover design: Laura Maitner-Mason
Cover photography: Leslie Aggar / Trevillion Images
Interior design: Katherine Lloyd

Printed in the United States of America

10 11 12 13 14 /DCI/ 22 21 20 19 18 17 16 15 14 13 12 11 10 9 8 7 6 5 4 3 2 1

To my father, Ralph Corn,
my husband, Stacy,
and our son, Brady —
three good men especially dear to me

Contents

Preface

*I*t's a bit ironic that we live in an age in which we are bombarded with sexual images, the topic of sex is tossed about easily in conversations, and the experience of pleasure is considered a right. And yet—and yet, the meaning in sexuality has been nearly lost.

Sexuality is a door that opens onto the richest secrets of your being, a purpose for your life that is larger than you. Simply put, any notions about sex will lead you to God in short order—and to the meaning of your life as a woman. That's why it's such a crucial quest. I hope this book will be one step on the road to the recovery of meaning for you.

As you read, I hope you will feel that you are in the midst of a spirited conversation about where relationships with men are meant to lead and what roles sex and sexuality are meant to play in your life. I'd hope this book seems like one long cup of coffee with someone who cares. We are sexually broken people—you, me, all of us. It's a given. Perhaps this book will become a door into something more, something different, something healing.

Hours and hours of listening to women tell their stories have formed this book. As I have listened to woman after woman describe the impact on her life of broken sexual bonds, I have been struck by how much of her real self she loses in this experience—often at an age before she even begins to come into her own. It's like seeing a house with the lights on inside and the windows boarded up. So little light, so little life, shines out from within. Being parceled out sexually to too many men takes a toll on the spirit.

When I listen to such stories, I sense a tiny sliver of the grief God feels—the God who created woman in his own image, with life-giving potential. Yet while I sense God's grief, I also gain fresh appreciation for the power of Christ and the wonder of the gospel to restore our actual selves. I am reminded of Jesus' words: "Very truly I tell you, everyone who sins is a slave to sin. Now a slave has no permanent place in the family, but a son belongs to it forever. So if the Son sets you free, you will be free indeed."[1] Ultimately, only the One who made us can set us free.

Let me say a few words about how to use this book in a group setting. The discussion of past sexual experiences in a group can be an enormously healing thing—but only if there is *confidentiality* and *freedom*. You will want to make sure everyone has agreed to keep what is spoken in that group right there—in that group. Similarly, if there are any questions at the end of the chapter that feel too revealing in a group setting, then feel the total freedom to say, "I pass on that question." Since the topic is sexuality, it's especially helpful to close any group session in prayer.

So, welcome. Fasten your seat belt. I think you will find this to be a good ride, an insightful journey, a helpful process, and maybe even a new beginning.

—Paula Rinehart
April 2010

Sex is responsible for most of the ecstasies on the planet, but it is also responsible for lots of murders and suicides. It is the most powerful of all fires, the most dangerous of all fires, and the fire which, ultimately, lies at the base of everything, including the spiritual life.

–RONALD ROLHEISER

1

Longing for Love

If he wants her just for her body, that splits her. It means that she is good to him only for a part of her. That's why when she's slept with him, she wants to know where the relationship is headed. She wants to be integrated. She craves it. She wants to know that he will be there in the morning, and the next morning, and the next morning. She wants to know that beyond the sex, he loves her, he wants her—all the time.

—Rob Bell

Sometimes I sit in the darkened theatre of a good chick-flick fighting the strangest urge to take off my shoe and throw it at the screen. I appreciate the great story line—and I love a good laugh. I recognize this is a timeless, engaging tale being told here: a guy meets a girl, and something mysterious clicks between them, something that hints of at least the possibility of forever.

But an inch into my popcorn—or about fifteen minutes into the film (I time these things), the predictable usually happens. This man and woman fall into bed together. It's the most natural thing in the world, and only to be expected in our enlightened day. These things happen, you know. And if, heaven forbid, there's some twist in the story and this "relationship" doesn't work out—well, both parties just go on. On to the next romantic possibility.

They go on unscathed, unharmed, without the slightest backward glance of sexual regret.

This illusion that men and women can join their selves by joining their bodies and nothing is altered on a deeper soul level is like thinking you can tramp around on the Great Barrier Reef in your mask and fins and the plant life will remain undisturbed. It's an illusion that doesn't match real life. And it's this illusion that leaves me fighting the urge to take off my shoe and throw it at the movie screen.

I want to stand up in the middle of the aisle and shout, "Stop! Could we tell the truth for once? Would somebody please tell the real story?"

I think someone needs to tell something a little closer to the truth. Which is why I'm writing this book. Of course, you have every right to ask what would make me privy to the real story. How would I know that what's on that movie screen doesn't match the actual lives of people? How am I aware of the pain and loss and regret, especially for women, in the experience of being joined—and then unjoined—to men who came and went?

By the nature of my work, I hear what women say the morning after, the month after, or even five years later. As a therapist, I hear the stories, especially the stories women tell, when they realize they lost something in this encounter with a man, some piece of themselves they fear they can't get back. In a guy's arms, a woman feels so powerfully wanted, like someone is waving a magic wand for a moment over her insecurities and they evaporate. Only the sense of being wanted can turn to ashes—and the insecurities, well, those take on a life of their own.

No one wants to storyboard the truth. *Sex outside its intended bonds is as destructive and soul tearing as it is healing and redemptive inside the bonds it's meant for.* Or to use an earlier metaphor: There's no way to tramp around on the Great Barrier Reef in your fins without disturbing the beautiful plant life there. It's just not the way nature—or relationships—work.

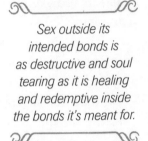

Sex outside its intended bonds is as destructive and soul tearing as it is healing and redemptive inside the bonds it's meant for.

THE STORIES WOMEN ACTUALLY TELL

Carol gathers her clothes off the floor, tiptoeing silently around the bedroom in the early dawn, hoping not to wake this man. Snoring in quiet, even rhythm, it will be hours before he gets up. When he can, he likes to sleep until noon, and she has a ton of stuff to do today. Besides, it's easier to slip back into her place before her roommates awaken—fewer raised eyebrows and sly smiles to contend with that way.

Driving back to her apartment, Carol muses over how their relationship began. Who ever would have thought that cochairing a political committee would lead to this? They began as good friends, challenging each other's opinions with an occasional lighthearted jab. But one thing led to another, and after a few months, she began to stay over at his place. It made for less hassle. How or when or where the relationship turned sexual, she isn't sure. She just knows that she is starting to have feelings for this guy, and that this could be a problem.

There are no guarantees in relationships now. How many times have her friends drilled that into her? "You just have to go with the flow" is the mantra she hears. "Don't say much; don't ask for anything. Just play it cool and see where the relationship goes."

The problem is that Carol has already done this twice before.

These are the kinds of stories that women tell. Perhaps you can hear the uncertainty ringing in Carol's story. The expectation is that she'll take the pleasure of the moment and keep her heart out of the picture. She's got to chop herself up in pieces to go forward. But there is no "forward" that she can rightfully look for without being seen as the needy, pushy woman. From this way of doing relationships, it's so easy to drift from one to the next to the next—with little pieces of your self scattered hither and yon.

Something cataclysmic is happening in the sexual lives of women today. A breathtaking amount of change has come about in one short generation. A man and woman fall into bed together with no promises made and no expectations to which they can hold each other. What I hope will become apparent as you read is that this road doesn't lead anywhere you really want to go. And it's possible—really possible—to get back what you've lost and to experience relationships with men much differently.

I begin with the comforting reality that, regardless of our age or background, we are all telling the same story—of losses that are difficult to absorb, fears that keep us awake at night, and dreams that have been incubating in us since we were quite small. We are all fundamentally the same.

It's just that the particular shape of women's stories now is deeply influenced by their sexual experiences. The loosening of sexual boundaries—the pressure to be sexual—plots our course in life in noticeable ways. Perhaps you recognize stories like these:

- Shannon is desperate for something that will curb the panic attacks that descend on her unannounced. Her job as a news reporter is being threatened by these sweaty emotional monsters. Shannon has just broken up with a man named Ben—a great guy she met last year in college and followed to the city, where they both landed their first jobs. She feels bad about beginning to sleep with Ben a few years ago. It violated her convictions as a Christian, but she developed her own way of justifying their sexual relationship. At least it was better than many women around her. This was no one-night fling— she and Ben were planning a future together.

  Two things caught Shannon by surprise. She hadn't anticipated that her growing attachment to Ben would be met with a reaction of his own—she was slowly caricatured as this woman "with too much of a hold on him." The more attached she became, the more detached he got—until she finally wanted out altogether. And Shannon had no idea that leaving Ben after this investment of herself would feel like a miniature divorce.

- Donna says she has always been sexually curious. Movies she saw in middle school, stories of her older siblings' late-night capers, and easy access to soft porn left her primed for her own sexual adventures. When a boy showed interest in her, it was she who upped the ante, moving things to the next level of sexual intimacy. By the time she left high school, she had been with a good number of guys.

  Now, in her second year of college, Donna finally has begun to wonder where her sexual activity is headed. What is the point? she asks. Why does she feel numb inside—as though her body is disconnected from the rest of her? Donna watches other couples and wonders if she will ever know what it feels like to have a man love her—just for her. A vague sense of regret and loss she cannot name follows her around. She longs to retrace her steps and find the innocence of soul she once knew.

- Emily's introduction to her own sexuality came from the most injurious of all possible routes. Her favorite brother used to slip into her room at night, just as she was turning twelve, where he held her in his arms and fondled her changing body. The bittersweet experience of hating yourself while you enjoyed intimacy never meant to be was profoundly ingrained in Emily's psyche. Being date-raped in high school just seemed like one more act in a bad play. With the sexual walls in her life broken down, Emily accepted the terms of the inevitable: a relationship with a man comes with a sexual price tag. Sex is part of the dues you pay to keep the relationship—and she has had quite a few of those. The fog and pain after each breakup leads to one poor choice in men after another.

Emily feels as though she steps in and out of two lives. On Sunday mornings she plays the flute in a worship ensemble. She sincerely wants to follow God, but her sexual life feels out of her control. She can't reconcile her lifestyle with her beliefs about God.

In any direction you turn now, women feel not just the opportunity, but the pressure, to be sexual. I am sure the checkout lane in your grocery store looks just like mine. On any given day, I can reach for at least two magazines that will give me the latest tip on how to "do" a man—as though sex is assumed between two mature adults, as though it is a woman's job to provide the best experience possible. As though a woman should be able to shield her heart while she bares her body on cue. All of us—Christian and non—find ourselves swimming in the same cultural soup. We cannot help but be affected.

I hear similar stories in any part of the country. When I speak at seminars for women almost anywhere, they say the same things. *I was swept into major sexual experiences early on, before I even knew what was happening.* Women often feel like they've sexually traded little bits of their soul they can't get back. *I was so afraid I'd lose this guy that I felt like I had to have sex with him.* It's hard to hold a line when a woman senses a guy can get what he wants from three other women if she refuses.

Women are paying a tremendous price for the loosening of sexual boundaries—in broken hearts, in lost time, in a confused sense of self.

A LONGING FOR ROMANCE

Wouldn't you secretly love for a guy to break his neck to get to know you—just because you are an interesting woman to get to know? Wouldn't it spell amazing freedom to explore the different facets of a person without that process being preempted by the intensity of sex?

There's a growing awareness that something beautiful between men and women is being lost in the rush to be sexual.

That's actually the basis for the kind of love and romance that lasts.

In survey after survey, women say they miss the sense of romance, of being pursued by a man just for themselves. There's a growing awareness that something beautiful between men and women is being lost in the rush to be sexual. Some call it "lost civility." The notion that a woman is a prize in her own right, worth crossing the dance floor of life to get to know deeply, is no longer assumed. Indeed, the "death of romance" we are experiencing now has become a universal moan among women.

As I wrote this book and talked with women from other eras, I was blown away by the tales I heard—of dancing the night away in ball gowns and tuxedos on the Carolina coast with no thought of climbing into the same bed at dawn, of having a man ride the train for a day to spend a few hours with you. So much more was required of a man.

Perhaps the most engaging story that came my way, though, sheds some light on the respect and gentleness men and women tended to offer each other even if they never married. Charlotte, a lovely, silver-haired woman in her seventies, told me how she fell in love with a man she met on a slow boat to Europe while she was in college. They had hours to talk, watching the way the stars shine when there is only sky and sea. Frank continued to write after she returned home; he even came to see her once or twice. But she knew, as she had always known, that she would marry Joe, a man in her hometown whom she had dated for a couple of years. When Charlotte married a year later, out of kindness she sent Frank an invitation to the wedding. He replied with a gift—a leather-bound, early edition of John Milton's classic, his calling card tellingly stuck between the pages of *Paradise Lost*.

I share this simply to note that there is a connection between the romance and "being treated well" that we long for—and the sexual boundaries we have lost.

In the 1960s, the door into sexual experience got blown off its hinges. It seemed to be where all the happy people lived. It was like we thought we had invented sex. C. S Lewis remarked once that sex is such a sublime experience who would ever think it produced babies. And for the first time in history, it didn't. A woman could take a pill, and her worries of getting pregnant were next to nil. The consequences of sleeping together did not arrive in nine months wrapped in a soft blanket, crying for his mama. Other consequences were present, of course — but they went underground, deep into the realm of soul and spirit, where the damage is much harder to calculate.

People have been sleeping around, in and out of the wrong beds, since the dawn of time. The difference is that they knew to blush. When I pledged a college sorority in the 1960s, plenty of girls slept around and no one would pretend otherwise. But that behavior was discreet and accompanied by guilt and shame. My daughter pledged the same sorority twenty-five years later. Her virginity was so distinctive that her sorority sisters nicknamed her "Mary," as in the mother of Jesus. (She is blessed, thankfully, with a fairly thick skin.)

Campus life, almost anywhere now, has become a four-year immersion experience in every nuance of sexual freedom. A woman can't act shocked when a man in a towel emerges from her roommate's door — nor question why it might be a different guy than the one two weeks before. The stereotype of a well-adjusted coed is a woman who plays a sport, has a crack professional internship possibility, steers a campus committee, volunteers to mentor a homeless child — and enjoys avid sexual experiences with the men who come her way. It's another "skill" she has acquired. That she would feel hurt or betrayed when a man moves on is a sign of weakness. This is the first cardinal rule: She is not supposed to *attach*.

With this as a backdrop, it's easy as Christians to feel that our sexual "slipups" are less grievous by comparison. Maybe we aren't sleeping around with random people — but the sexual experience we engage in outside of marriage with someone we may even hope to marry still affects us. It never works to compartmentalize our sexual lives from our spiritual lives. Our sexuality—as well as our experience of God—is lived from our core.

So we long for love and romance because that's the way God made us. But love and romance are inextricably tied to courage. A man takes a deep breath and walks across the room to engage a woman without any guarantee that his ego will be stroked by a sexual payoff. Love and romance are built on a breathtakingly risky "giving of self" that asks for nothing that isn't ours to ask for.

OUT OF THE ASHES … HOPE

When I hear the stories that emerge from the sexual lives of women now and I sense the lack of self-respect, the blow to their dignity, the choices in men made out of a fog of pain and loss, a deep note of grief resounds within me. I find myself wanting to protest, "You are meant to be loved and valued and cherished for the rest of your life by a man whose face lights up when he sees you." Whether a woman marries or not, strength and respect are her God-given birthright. You can find the door out of destructive relationships with men and recover the parts of your heart and soul you may feel you've lost. It's entirely possible.

Considering what it has meant to grow up in a sexually charged culture with many of the natural barriers torn down, what kind of longings are stirred as you think about where you are in your relationships with men and where you would like to be? Those longings are so important. I love the way journalist Danielle Crittenden puts this: "The desire to be pursued and courted, to have sex with someone you love as opposed to just barely know, to be certain of a man's affection and loyalty—these are deep female cravings that did not vanish with the sexual revolution."[1]

Beneath the ashes of our pasts lies a golden core—the intrinsic, transcendent reality of being created in the very image of God as a woman.

The desire for romance and the beauty of a good relationship, for deep connections with people that last through thick and thin, is like a homing device that God installs in our hearts early on. Unless we have completely short-circuited, this is the very desire that will lead us home, in the most real sense of the word.

All real change of direction in our lives comes this way: We get a vision of what God has made us to experience, and we begin to walk toward that. Sometimes it's the pain we've experienced that drives us down a new path. Sometimes it's an intuitive sense that much more is possible in relationships with men. Perhaps the sexual connections we've made with men in our pasts are bleeding over into our ability to give our hearts to the right man now.

As women, we are designed for deep and lasting attachment—as someone's daughter, mother, aunt, sister, friend, or wife. No matter what we achieve or accomplish, our lives are empty without relationships of duration and depth.

Fundamentally, it is this life of relationship that the sexual insanity of our day so threatens. Relationships, especially those between men and women, are inherently hard to sustain. They require every part of you—mind and body and soul—intact and capable of committing *your heart* into the safekeeping of another.

I invite you to explore the world of your sexuality in ways that perhaps you never have—to consider the power and beauty God pours out on you as a woman. Your sexual experience with men may be as pure as the driven snow. Or you may have known enough shame and heartache to fill a book. The good news is that beneath the ashes of our pasts lies a golden core—the intrinsic, transcendent reality of being created in the very image of God as a woman. If we listen to the longings of the heart God gave us, we will find our way home.

Questions for Discussion and Reflection

1. When do you feel not just the opportunity but the pressure to be sexual with a man? How do you feel about this?

2. What would more romance in a relationship look like from your perspective?

3. When does it seem like it's just too much to hope that a relationship with a man could really work out without sex being part of the picture? What effect does the refusal to hope have on relationships? On life as a whole?

4. If a woman remains single, yet moves from one sexual relationship to another, what will be the impact on her?

5. In terms of a "deep and lasting attachment" to a man, what qualities are you looking for in him? In the relationship itself?

2

What Women Lose

That women may actually be the losers in the sexual revolution is an idea just dawning on this generation of young women, who feel as sexually free as it is possible to feel and yet are so often powerless to experience anything more with the opposite sex than unsatisfying, loveless flings.

—Danielle Crittenden

he woman I am listening to slides back on the sofa, adjusting her skirt as though preparing for an important interview. Claire is a lovely woman about thirty years old, married to a man she met a couple of years ago in the law firm where she works. She is not happy about being in a counselor's office, but she has to talk to somebody. There is tension in her marriage, and she's scared.

I ask her to tell me about the problem, which, of course, could be any number of things.

"Well," she starts in slowly, "it's sex. The problem is that I hate sex."

Occasionally I talk to a woman who is just plain honest—no fuss, no hedging, no effort to clean up a dirty elephant. *I hate sex.* I hear this statement often these days.

Claire goes on to describe why she finds this part of her life so disagreeable. It's boring; she's been there before; she feels a trifle used—though she's not sure where this feeling comes from. She and her husband became Christians a few years ago, and she hoped this would change her feelings about sex, but it hasn't. "I could live my whole life and never miss sex." She almost whispers the words. She feels so guilty. After all, she's only thirty. Her husband is tired, not of sex, but of her disinterest. He hints that he can't live like this—not feeling wanted sexually by his wife. Claire is beginning to panic.

Somewhere in this conversation, Claire starts to turn the pages of her life back ten years. She begins to talk about the first time she had sex.

"I didn't want to have a bad experience in losing my virginity—like some of my friends," she says. "So I found a guy I didn't feel anything special for, and I had sex with him. That way I could just get it over with."

"Losing your virginity was something you wanted to just get over?" I think I must have heard Claire wrong.

"Well, sure. That way I wouldn't get hurt, or so I thought. Then maybe I would enjoy sex with guys I really cared about."

Somehow things didn't go according to plan. Sex became something Claire did to keep a relationship with a guy. Over the years, there were a lot of guys, including the man she eventually married. She loves him, but sex is stuck in the place it began for her. She knows it should be different now that she is married.

"On my honeymoon, I could feel the jail bars coming down," Claire confesses. She saw herself facing a lifetime of feeling reluctant and used. She just hadn't expected that it would affect the overall health of her marriage this much.

$$\rightsquigarrow$$

Sometimes it takes a while for a woman to feel the weight of sexual relationships with men she has known. After all, we live in a culture determined to minimize this impact. Sex is supposed to be one more pleasure to be had between a man and a woman. The emotional aftermath is usually swept under the rug.

The truth is often much closer to Claire's story. She knows sex with her husband should be full of joy and sweet abandonment. But it brings up feelings she didn't even know she had. Memories she had long forgotten.

New psychological research underscores the impact of first sexual experiences. *Psychology Today* senior editor Jay Dixit writes, "Intense emotional sensations etch first experiences deeply into memory, creating what psychologists call 'flashbulb memories.'" Dixit quotes psychologist Susan Anderson: "Powerful first relationships can stamp a template in your mind that gets activated in later interactions."[1] It's like the brain records the experience of first sex or first love on an inerasable tape.

A woman often feels the effect of broken sexual bonds

more deeply than she ever thought she would. Yes, it takes two to tango, but sex outside marriage is usually harder on women.

That's not fair! you say, and I totally agree. But there are solid reasons why we feel the impact more.

You can see the reality of this mirrored in the physical dimension. A woman is far more likely to contract a sexually transmitted disease than the man she sleeps with. The most prevalent viral STD is human papillomavirus (HPV), a major cause of cervical cancer in women. Sexually transmitted diseases in women often operate like a stealth bomber, remaining silent and invisible for years. The symptoms are internal and hidden, where they are harder to detect, surfacing years later. The heart is not unlike the body. As Claire discovered, her heart had been bruised more than she would have guessed by her earlier sexual life.

Part of the explanation for the "deeper impact" lies in our basic makeup. A woman is wired for connection. Like the original Eve, whose name means "mother of the living," our identity is about giving life, having connection with others. We have this wonderful ability to foster life and relationship. So being in and out of relationships is incongruent with our deepest selves. It's simply not the way God made women.

The words I just wrote would have been loudly booed a few years back. They are still considered politically incorrect. But few knowledgeable people dispute them now — not after the latest rounds of brain and hormone research.

The reality is that the delicate interplay of hormones and the structure of your brain provide ample reason for relationships being central to you as a woman. For the first two years of your life and again during puberty, your brain is marinated in estrogen. That reality, combined with a larger hippocampus, means that you pick up people cues and put words to feelings staggeringly better than a guy. You are hard-wired for connection—and to feel that this connection matters. So when a relationship falls apart, that registers too. The normal sadness anyone would feel affects six times as many neurons in the brain of a woman than a man. The common expression, then, that a woman just "feels more deeply" (a statement often made accusingly) has an actual physiological basis.[2]

So you can understand that when a woman asks a counselor to help her learn how to be with men sexually and walk away and not be upset (which is what she perceives a man does), a counselor just shakes her head. It's like asking for a lobotomy.

You are designed to bring a special capacity for ever-increasing levels of depth and intimacy into a relationship with a man. It's one of the best qualities God gave to you as a woman. It's tragic to have that capacity for relationship diminished because your ability to trust is so bruised—but this is what many women experience.

Everything in a woman cries out for a relationship that endures. She is much less able to love a man and then leave him. For that macabre feat, she must be taught. The message that she should be able to walk off unaffected, as a man supposedly does, must be drilled into her. It does not come naturally. And as we will see in the last chapter, broken sexual bonds have their own negative effects in the lives of men.

EMOTIONAL SCARRING

I can tell you as a therapist that it's hard work (for all the reasons above) to help a woman get through a painful breakup with a man. It's hard almost to the degree that she's been sexually involved with him. As one social commentator noted recently, "Getting over a relationship takes twice the time of the relationship itself. Women describe their post-breakup period like a flu bug that is hard to shake."[3] Danielle Crittenden explains the phenomenon:

> All the sexual bravado a girl may possess evaporates the first time a boy she truly cares for makes it clear that he has no further use for her after his own body has been satisfied. No amount of feminist posturing, no amount of reassurances that she doesn't need a guy like that anyway, can protect her from the pain and humiliation of those awful moments after he's gone, when she's alone and feeling not sexually empowered but discarded.[4]

Again, men don't escape the pain, but you won't see many of them agonizing in introspection, searching for their hidden flaws that must have surely, somehow, caused this breakup.

I have found that women more often ask the painful question, "What's wrong with me?" Physical intimacy feels like an investment of one's self. Thus, leaving or being left prompts a good deal of self-doubt and second-guessing. One's naked self feels exposed and unwanted. For many women, it is hard to pull out of this downward, introspective spiral. Even when a woman regains her objectivity, she still feels that it is a huge risk to enter into another relationship. She asks, "How much of my heart am I willing to trust a man with?" She measures out tiny bits of herself, reluctantly, never letting anyone get too close.

From this impossible bind, a woman often moves into another relationship she later regrets. She thinks, *I will find a man who appreciates me*. She chooses a safe man, but one hardly worthy of her affection. *I will find a man who won't leave me*. She accepts the attention of a man, ignoring glaring, red warning signals: He's thoughtless, inconsiderate, too often looking out for his own interests. But he's not going to leave. The pain of prying a woman apart from a man with whom she has bonded sexually can be wrenching and blinding for some time to come.

One of the hidden repercussions of combining sex and relationships is the way a woman can learn to step out of her body. It's a fairly easy maneuver. You just send your body out to relate to a man, but the real you floats in space somewhere essentially unconnected. Your body may experience pleasure, but you have stepped out of the moment. When things fall apart, you aren't affected as deeply — or so it seems. Sadly, this is nearly the

Dabbling in the promiscuous can lock many wonderful things about sex in the realm of the illicit.

exact same dynamic by which a woman can stay in an abusive relationship for a long time. Pretending rises to the level of an art form. She gets so used to stepping out of her body that she doesn't attend to the way she's being treated. As in Claire's story, it's an emotional "skill" learned in multiple sexual encounters.

Perhaps you are asking at this point how a lifestyle of having sex with guys can become a setup for abusive relationships with men. It's a fair question. The best explanation is in the nature of the sexual experience itself. When sexual intimacy happens inside the bonds of a marriage, both parties have given up a measure of their independence in order to take on a real responsibility for the other person. Or as the common expression goes, *marriage is an assault on selfishness*. And this, again, is God's design.

But if you lift the sexual piece out of marriage and make it a stand-alone experience, grounded simply in pleasure, then sex becomes a commodity. A "thing." More like exchanging a sack of groceries. It's only a short distance, then, to being treated like a sack of groceries rather than a real woman with needs who deserves to be cherished. A woman who exchanges sex for what (feels like) love signs an emotional contract with a guy that can slowly turn flat-out abusive. It's actually the same inner contract that a prostitute signs, only the terms are clearer: She accepts money in exchange for her body.

Even if relationships don't turn abusive, though, a woman still finds that dabbling in the promiscuous can lock many wonderful things about sex in the realm of the illicit. On the far side of marriage, she may feel that the excitement and playfulness meant to accompany married sex seems strangely off-limits. The struggle to decontaminate her present experience, to reclaim what she knows is meant for good, can be enormous.

LOSS OF THE TRUE FEMININE

Have you noticed how much being a woman is trumpeted—until she starts to feel something messy? Like pain, regret, anger, disappointment, jealousy that she has given herself sexually to a man and then, boom, the relationship is over, for example. Heaven forbid that she should be upset.

It's really a new form of misogyny, this denial of feelings. A woman isn't supposed to feel anything. Not fear that her current relationship may not last. Not grief when it's over. Not a bit of tacky resentment when another woman comes into the picture. To feel something—to be hurt, betrayed, devastated—would be to admit that she had hopes and expectations at the outset. This is a big taboo. What would ever give her the idea that sex meant something or that her sexual favors were valuable? She should be able to walk away and expect nothing. The proof of our equality with men has become our ability to flatline a broken heart. As Wendy Shalit writes:

> All those bad feelings we are too enlightened to feel nowadays—such as resentment, jealousy, betrayal—also signify the capacity to lose yourself in the first place, to fall in love with someone other than yourself. They presuppose that there is a soul to protect, that there are hopes to be shattered, a lost love to guard, even if now only mentally and futilely. No hard feelings? I'm advocating a return to precisely that: hard feelings. At least then you know you're a person, that you have a heart.[5]

Oddly enough, as Shalit observes, it is the pain we feel when sexual bonds are made and broken that reminds us we were made for more. God made women to experience the joy of lasting, enduring relationships with men. That we cannot deaden our heart successfully is the best apologetic I know for the truth of how God made us.

Unfortunately, most of us turn these potent feelings back on ourselves. We think, *I need to be less sensitive. If I could only keep my heart from getting involved. There must be something wrong with me.* In a culture that trivializes everything transcendent, a woman's passionate nature is a bit embarrassing and, well, somehow bad.

This is really an effort to cure womanhood as though it were an illness, as Shalit points out. We can handle a woman starving herself into a size 4. A woman who demands the pay raise she's due is roundly admired. We can deal with her. But a real, living woman with hopes and dreams, with an unveiled longing for a good man and a child to tuck in at night—what does our culture say to her?

She needs to get some tear-proof mascara and a good antidepressant.

Maybe it's just the other way around, which is to say we aren't crazy. Shalit writes:

> Maybe it is normal for a young woman to be "intense" and being cavalier is what is strange. Maybe wanting to forge bonds with others is normal, and it's cutting ourselves off from enduring attachments that is perverse. Maybe *not* having "rejection sensitivity" is what is sick, and *in*vulnerability to loss the real pathology.

If being blasé about sex were natural, why would so many women have to be on Prozac in order to carry out what their culture expects of them?[6]

HOW SEX BECOMES AN ADDICTION

Do you remember how Madonna traded on her sexuality and made herself into a cultural icon?

Her biographer notes that she could hold an audience of eighty thousand people spellbound. Yet one of her former lovers claims that, privately, Madonna is the most insecure woman he has ever known. "She remains at heart the little girl continually trying to win over her father, searching for love and acceptance," he says.[7] How does a woman so successful remain so young and insecure inside, like she's frozen at fifteen?

Madonna is a picture writ large of the emotional bargain that women strike with their sexuality. It's a familiar cycle, the easiest pattern in the world to follow. A girl realizes she has something a guy is desperate for. And if she trades something sexual with a guy, he gives some of the emotional validation and sense of worth she is equally desperate for. Only both parties lose out. Their respective need grows; the hole of insecurity gets larger. In a sexual encounter, it's rarely the ultimate orgasm that a woman is after. What hooks her is the feeling of being loved, wanted, valued in the warm embrace of some man's arms.

This can get to be a kind of relational cocaine. A woman gets to a place where she just can't turn down the possibility of the sexual, emotional stroke that being with a man gives.

Even when she knows ahead of time she will hate herself in the morning. This is the bondage of a sexual addiction. Being alone or being without a man can be the hardest thought in the world. "No, I'd rather not" feels like the ticket to the back side of the desert.

And it all begins with the cycle of that simple exchange: I'll give you some of my body in exchange for the feeling of being loved.

Now here's the irony. The deeper a woman gets into the almost compulsive need for the sexual validation of a man, the more she needs to be alone. Herself. And OK with herself, which is often a conclusion she slowly comes to as she gets more connected to God and to people who love her—all of her and not just her body.

So I find myself in conversations with a woman struggling with what you can only call an addiction. I invite her to dry out from the world of men—especially the world of alcohol and men. I describe what celibacy can actually do for her that nothing else can, really. I know it sounds like a prison sentence. But, in reality, it's her get-out-of-jail-free card. It's exactly like the picture Jesus painted. "Enter through the narrow gate," he said, even though it's harder and there aren't many people lined up in front.[8] But that narrow gate opens up on the other side to Life—to this wide, expansive place with a thousand possibilities of really being loved. And the broad gate? That's where the crowd is, laughing and partying like the party will go on forever.

But the broad gate actually leads to a narrow place, tight and constricted, with precious few choices remaining. Which is the very essence of being in the grip of an addiction. Only that one thing matters. And she will exchange her life to have it.

In his book *Sex God*, author Rob Bell explains addiction as the biblical progression of lust. Lust deadens us on the inside. We lose the ability to feel things like we used to. This loss of sensitivity and true enjoyment, then, leads to what the Bible calls being "given over to sensuality."[9] Our appetites become insatiable. Bell writes, "Whether it's food, sex, shopping, whatever, what was supposed to fill the hole within us didn't. It betrayed us. It owns us. And it always leaves us wanting more."[10]

THE NEED TO RECLAIM

A woman waits to talk with me after I have finished speaking in a seminar. She seems unusually patient, letting everyone else go in front of her, as though she is saving something for my ears alone.

She begins by telling me how her life recently has taken such a good turn. In her own words, she says she has found faith for the first time. She smiles when she tells me this. A relationship with God is something she ran from for many years, but no more. Life is opening up on the inside of her, and she loves this. What she sees in this new light is how much she keeps people—men especially—at arm's length. Only so close and no closer. This troubles her.

She pours out her story. She lost her father when she was ten years old. They were in a car accident together, and she alone survived. She remembers the doctor and her mother coming to her hospital bedside to tell her that her father had died in surgery. She says she could feel a hole as big as her dad himself opening up inside her.

The first guy to pay her some attention was a junior in her geography class. She was a freshman. He had shoulders like two goal posts, and as he began to single her out, she felt better than she had for a long time. As spring moved into summer, she gave in to his persistent demand for sex. She didn't want to lose him or the feeling of specialness he gave her. But within weeks, he had picked up with another girl. He moved through her friends like he was sampling a box of chocolates. A year or so later, he admitted that her actual appeal to him had been her innocence. *Her innocence.*

"Where did you go from this relationship?" I asked her quietly. What I heard knotted up my insides. She had moved from this slap in the face to a string of guys, one after the other, for the next seven years. "What difference does it make now?" she reasoned. Her hunger for a guy to fill the void grew like kudzu in a swamp.

"Which of these guys treated you well? Have you known what it feels like to be really cared for by any man since your father died?" I asked, one question atop the other.

A little trail of tears slid down her cheek—a wordless, resounding no.

Many of us give away something precious before we know what we have. No one in our lives alerts us to our vulnerability; no one values our sexuality enough to struggle for its protection. Or perhaps we do not allow ourselves to hear someone who wants to help.

Like Claire at the beginning of this chapter, many of us found that early feelings of sexual pleasure that seemed mildly illicit mutated into the fear of leaving or of being left. Now, though we are older and may be married, the thrill is gone. Perhaps, more accurately, the passion got diluted like a sexual dam that burst and spread water an inch deep over a wide field when it was meant to be a powerful river to nurture and sustain us for a lifetime.

For almost any woman who looks back over the debris of her sexual past, there is a measure of loss and regret. So much she wishes she could redo — or undo. The voice of one woman in her late twenties continues to haunt me. In wisdom beyond her years, she said, "I wish I hadn't given so much of myself. I feel that some of my experiences *thinned my soul*, and such an effect takes time to undo."[11] This thinning of the soul, of our capacity to enter into life and relationship with all we are, is perhaps the greatest loss of all.

> Grief is what tells you that you were meant for more, that God made your body and your soul to be inextricably joined.

I focus on the genuine sense of loss that goes with the territory of sexual bonds made and broken outside the parameters of marriage. For, strangely enough, grief is what tells you that you were meant for more, that God made your body and your soul to be inextricably joined. Grief reminds you that you are human, and that after all is said and done, you still have not managed — thank God — to amputate your heart. The first step to reclaiming anything of value is to be able to name the pain.

In this grief, we are not merely victims. No, our grief is

the result of choices we have made. Perhaps, though, we are ready for someone to connect the emotional dots—to see our longing for an enduring relationship as something that is rightfully ours, something meant to be. The pain has meaning.

Perhaps, despite all the hype to the contrary, we actually long for someone to remind us of the beauty and passion and tender strength that are possible in a relationship with a man. A good man. Perhaps we are ready to let God do what only he can do, which is to restore us from the inside out.

Questions for Discussion and Reflection

1. Do you agree that women pay a stiffer price than men in the making and breaking of sexual bonds? Why or why not?

2. Where in this culture do you observe the insistence that you should be able to be sexually involved with a guy and not be emotionally attached?

3. What are some of the conclusions you have drawn out of the pain of a failed relationship? How do you see those conclusions now?

4. When, in a relationship, do you feel used or sense you are in some way "using" someone else to meet your own needs?

3

A Woman's Power

Women control not the economy of the marketplace but the economy of eros: the life force in our society and our lives. What happens in the inner realm of women finally shapes what happens on our social surfaces, determining [our] level of happiness, energy, creativity, and solidarity.

– GEORGE GILDER

Like a solo rock star, [a male] must devise a bower, song, and dance that wows the gals. Among bowerbirds and most other animals as well, it's the females that do the choosing.

– NATIONAL GEOGRAPHIC

He has driven all afternoon under a hot August sun just to surprise Sandy a day early. It took some real sweet talking to convince his boss he could make up the time later. But it will be worth the trouble, he's sure. His friends all complain. Why is he so scarce, so much less available to them? The days of fishing or playing golf all weekend are fading into memory. Since Sandy appeared on the landscape of his life, he's been strangely preoccupied. He used to vow he'd never do one of those long-distance relationships. Until he met Sandy. Now he's standing on her front porch with a grin as wide as Texas.

⤻⚘

What lengths a guy will go to when he's set his sights on a particular woman! The power of a woman in a man's life is the theme of many a good movie or novel. Oh, to be the woman that some guy would drive clear across Texas to see.

Just this week, a big, tough policeman told me a story about the night he met an intriguing woman at a restaurant. They talked for hours, and after that he saw her every day for weeks. Meeting her changed his life. He stopped smoking pot, broke off with his partying friends, and married her one year later. And he never looked back. "She's the best thing that ever happened to me," he confided.

God gives a woman a particular sort of power in a guy's life. You could call it beauty, but then you'd be tempted to think it was bound up in your physical appearance. When really, it's far more than that.

Talking about a woman's power, though, is not an easy topic these days. Women fly bombing sorties. We sit on professional boards. We get the choice seats in the best graduate programs. But in the intimate places of our lives, how are we supposed to think about power, especially sexual power? What do you do with the actual influence you have in a man's life?

I know you may not feel very powerful—but trust me,

you are. As someone who steps into the trenches of people's lives, I see the power of a woman up close. I catch a glimpse in the devastated look on a man's face when the woman he loves says she will not try again to make their relationship work. I hear a man admit his fear. No matter how hard he tries, he may not be enough of *something* this woman needs, and perhaps, just perhaps, she will prefer another man to him.

I watch the ease of an elderly couple sharing coffee at McDonald's, the utter at-homeness they exude, the tender way he reaches for her hand to help her cross the parking lot. I walk past a good friend's desk at work, the space crammed with family pictures—his wife and children at the beach, his son playing football, his wife on their twenty-fifth anniversary. And suddenly I realize what he is saying without words: "This is the reason I show up day after grinding day."

When I try to capture the mystery of it all, my mind turns to an amazing story out of World War II. On D-Day, thousands of Allied troops stormed the beaches of Normandy. Dying and wounded men lay everywhere. Army medics with bright red armbands attended them. But by a strange set of circumstances, a young French woman named Jacqueline was also there, having come to retrieve a bathing suit she'd left on the beach the day before. When she saw the carnage, she stayed for two whole days and nights to help.

Years afterward when the men who'd survived the invasion of Normandy gathered at reunions, they debated whether there had actually been a woman on the beach with them. Perhaps it had been an angel. Maybe it was a hallucination.

Jacqueline lived to be an old woman in a small French

village, and she reports that over the years, grateful veterans showed up unexpectedly at her door wanting to thank the woman they remember as though she appeared in a dream.

Hundreds of male medics on the beach that day risked their lives, yet no one seems to dream about them. There are no reports of streams of men seeking them out years later to discover their identity. The story begs a central question: What is it about the touch of a woman in a moment of trauma and pathos that registers so deeply—indeed, that seems like a visit from an angel?

Whatever this power of a woman is, it surely must be strong stuff.

WHERE THIS ATTRACTION IS MEANT TO LEAD

So here are the questions simplified: Why is a man attracted to a woman? What is the nature of this attraction?

Oddly enough, poets and artists get at the answers better than sheer logic. Do you remember, for example, the way Bruce Springsteen sang about the "secret garden" a woman possesses? He sings about the way a woman will let you into her heart, to remote parts of herself—if you are willing to pay the price. She will let you deep inside her, "but there's a secret garden she hides."[1] A woman who knows her beauty understands that she has something exceptionally valuable to give and something important to protect.

A woman who knows her beauty understands that she has something exceptionally valuable to give and something important to protect.

Or read one of William Butler Yeats's most-loved poems.

"When You Are Old" hints at what it looks like when a man has been able to let a woman's desirability guide him to the essence beyond his initial attraction. The voice is that of a man as he speaks to a woman he has known well for many years.

> *When you are old and gray and full of sleep*
>   *And nodding by the fire, take down this book,*
>   *And slowly read, and dream of the soft look*
> *Your eyes had once, and of their shadows deep;*
>
> *How many loved your moments of glad grace,*
>   *And loved your beauty with love false or true;*
>   *But one man loved the pilgrim soul in you,*
> *And loved the sorrows of your changing face.*

Wouldn't you like to hope that maybe, just maybe, some man out there would, years from now, still love the pilgrim soul in you? I know I would. Unless our heart is just beaten to a pulp, we long for a man who could love the sorrows of our changing face. It's right for us to long for this. And for a man, knowing a woman's beauty to its depth is what he is meant to desire deeply. This "secret garden" may not be something he ever truly realizes, but it is so appealing that he will spend the rest of his life in pursuit of it.

This provides one small but telling clue why the sexual relationship between a man and a woman is described biblically by the verb "to know." To know a woman was to be sexually intimate with her. This intimacy led in a hundred directions, unfolding layer after layer of endless possibility between two people. Conversely, "to lie with" a woman was just simply to have sex outside the constraints of marriage, and as such it was expressly condemned. It is as though God says a man can't just sample the beauty and go on and not pay a price.

So God puts in a man a longing for what you bring to him as a woman, something so *not him* that he feels far more complete with you in his life. An intelligent man knows this. Deep down, he knows he's on a great search for what's missing. "It is not good for a man to be alone."[2] This famous line is found in the opening pages of the Bible. It's so often quoted because it proves to be so true. Without a woman a man tends to wander through life untethered and at loose ends, lacking purpose.

This is what you bring to a potential relationship. It's why he's drawn to you instinctively. Your power is sexual in nature, but it's a kind of beauty that is more mysterious, more intrinsic, than a lovely face or body. I think John and Stasi Eldredge capture this well in their book *Captivating*:

> Whatever else it means to be feminine, it is depth and mystery and complexity with beauty as its very essence. Now, lest despair set in, let us say as clearly as we can:
>
> Every woman has a beauty to unveil.
>
> Every woman.
>
> Because she bears the image of God. She doesn't have to conjure it, go get it from a salon, have plastic surgery or breast implants. No, beauty is an *essence* that is given to every woman at her creation.[3]

THE SOURCE OF A WOMAN'S BEAUTY

It's comforting to realize that your innate attractiveness—your beauty—does not originate with you. As that truth sinks in deeply, you will be able to relax and enjoy being enjoyed by the men in your life. And that pleasure won't be reduced to something expressed sexually.

Your beauty finds its source in the heart of God, in his image invested in your being as a woman. Have you thought much about what it means to be created as a woman in God's image? You could spend the rest of your life exploring this reality and not get to the end of it. No greater validation of your soul—your very self—exists anywhere than the reality of having God's image imprinted in your being. You are because he is.

The Father, Son, and Holy Spirit exist in perfect unity without erasing their individual personalities. And when this triune God set out to make human beings, it took both male and female to adequately express what he is like. "Then God said, 'Let us make human beings in our image, to be like us.' ... So God created human beings in his own image. In the image of God he created them; *male and female he created them*."[4] The essence of gender is rooted in the Trinity itself.

You can understand, then, why Pope John Paul once remarked that the thing wrong with pornography is that it doesn't show enough of a woman. It doesn't reveal her as a woman made in the image of God.

God so values the feminine that he incorporates it into his very being. There are places in Scripture where God compares himself to a mother who cannot forget her child[5]—indeed, one name for God in the original Hebrew is the "many-breasted" one. Every member of the Trinity— Father, Son, and Holy Spirit—moves in compassion, gentle correction, and faithful presence, which are traits we commonly associate with the feminine. Rather than undervaluing the feminine, God hallows it.

Think of the earliest picture of a woman in the Genesis creation account. After God has brought light into darkness, after he has made everything from a giraffe to a whooping crane, God creates Adam—a man who bears his own image, distinct from all the animals around him. But God doesn't stop there. From Adam's side, God makes Eve. She is God's finishing touch, and all Adam can say is, "Wow!" "Eve embodies the beauty and mystery and tender vulnerability of God," writes John Eldredge. And then he quotes poet William Blake: "The naked woman's body is a portion of eternity too great for the eye of man."[6]

Eve stands as the pinnacle of God's creation. Or as Mike Mason put it in his classic book about the mystery of marriage:

> My wife's body is brighter and more fascinating than a flower, shier than any animal, and more breathtaking than a thousand sunsets. To me her body is the most awesome thing in creation. Trying to look at her, just trying to take in her wild, glorious beauty, so free and primal, so utterly unchanged since the beginning of time, I catch a small glimpse of what it means that men and women have been made in the image of God. If even the image is this dazzling, what must the Original be like?[7]

A CURIOUS POWER

From this mysterious essence, then, comes the particular power that women possess.

You can sense it in a variety of settings—in the way distinguished men stop and listen to a woman's intuitive hunch, or the instinctual way a man looks to a woman to provide an emotional sense of home and quiet refuge. But this "power" takes a particular form when it comes to the romantic dance between a man and a woman. And if we miss the importance of our power here, we will never be able to use it wisely.

Simply put, it is the power of yes and no. The delicate dance between a man and woman makes you the decision maker in whether or not—or when and how—a man's most urgent physical need will be met. You can name the stakes. And while it may not feel like much "power" to you, a man knows that other than resorting to rape, he is at your mercy. God rests enormous power in the heart of a woman. The most vulnerable aspect of a man's being requires your permission, your reception of him. God makes a woman the prize to be won—a prize that is meant to go to a man worthy of her. She becomes "the ultimate worldly arbiter of a man's worth."[8]

For most women, the power of female sexuality is something we can feel and sense, but it's not something we have really considered. We grasp, however, even less about the sexuality of men, particularly the vulnerability they face. Women are simply more sexually secure than men. Believe it or not, we really are.

"The prime fact of life is the sexual superiority of women,"

George Gilder wrote in one of the most telling books on men to date.[9] By this Gilder means that a woman's body gives her many profound, repeated clues to who she is, and to her worth as a woman. She can give birth and nurse children at her breast, amazing feats of creativity and accomplishment. A man is limited to one sexual act—intercourse—and for this act, he must perform. While a woman may or may not be into the sexual experience, if a man does not perform, it's "a showstopper," as they say. "For men," writes Gilder, "the desire for sex is not simply a quest for pleasure. It is an indispensable test of identity."[10]

The most vulnerable aspect of a man's being requires your permission, your reception of him.

For a man, there is simply more riding on this precarious venture called sexual intimacy. And this is yet another factor that tilts power in the direction of a woman. Gilder states:

> This difference between the sexes gives the woman the superior position in most sexual encounters. The man may push and posture, but the woman must decide. He is driven; she must set the terms and conditions, goals and destination of the journey. Her faculty of greater natural restraint and selectivity makes the woman the sexual judge and executive, finally appraising the offerings of men, favoring one and rejecting another, and telling them what they must do to be saved or chosen.[11]

The beauty, allure, and sexual power you hold as a woman are holy things. They can bless beyond your wildest dreams or, as the biblical writer of the ancient proverbs observed, destroy everything you hold dear.[12] The choice is yours. How will you use this power?

You can pull a man toward you, make him as compliant as a well-trained puppy, use your sexuality to seduce him, or to try to bind his heart to yours. Either party can manipulate the other. Or you can choose a slightly more challenging course. Your willingness to reserve sex for the context of marriage (conservative chic, if you will) translates into sexual power that buys you time and courage to consider the man before you. What is he really like? What are his intentions? What kind of future with you does he have in mind?

The sexual power, the mysterious beauty at a woman's disposal, is such strong stuff that God means for her to confine it to one arena — marriage. There it becomes part of the glue that bonds two people together, body and soul, for a lifetime.

A POWER EMBRACED

In the classic movie *Pretty Woman*, Julia Roberts gained instant fame as a small-town girl turned prostitute who falls in love with a man for whom she only meant to provide a paid service. It's the tale of a man who is transformed by love he never intended to feel.

One scene, in particular, is pivotal. You never forget it. Richard Gere has made Julia Roberts an offer that all logic would dictate she should accept. He will put her up in a classy condo and give her a running credit account to buy whatever she wants just so she will be there waiting for him when he comes to town. She will be his mistress.

But in the few weeks they've been together, Julia has changed. She has shed the self-image of a prostitute. Instead, she sees herself as a lovely woman, much more aware of what she has to offer a man. The "pretty woman" has realized her beauty. She tells Gere that when she was a little girl, her mother used to lock her in the attic when she was bad. She would pretend she was a princess in a tower, and a knight would come with his colors flying. She would wave, and he would climb the tower to rescue her. And then comes Julia's vintage line: "Never in all that time did the knight say, 'Honey, I'll put you up in a great condo.' A few months ago I could have taken your offer. Now everything is different. *I want more*" (emphasis mine).

I wonder how many of us long to say words just like that to a man. "No, I will not accept the crumbs under the table." How many of us are aware of wanting more—of longing for a man who sees in us a love he cannot do without? A man who does not insist on separating sex from marriage? How many of us long for the courage to just put it out there like Julia Roberts: *No, I want more?*

> When sex is an investment you make in the love of your life, it multiplies into a storehouse of pleasure and intimacy that blesses every other part of your life with a man.

To claim your true sexual power is to embrace the courage and strength of that statement. It means you refuse to squander this power by doling yourself out in bits and pieces in the relationship of the moment. Sexual power is right at the heart of who you are as a woman. It is power that is rightfully yours. When sex

is an investment you make in the love of your life, it multiplies
into a storehouse of pleasure and intimacy that blesses every
other part of your life with a man. That's what it was meant to
be—a rich joy stored up for you by the mercy of God.

This kind of power belongs to you innately. It is your
birthright. And yet, oddly enough, you will only be able to
experience its importance in a relationship when you have
first deeply embraced it for yourself.

Questions for Discussion and Reflection

1. Were you aware before reading this chapter that
   you, as a woman, have an innate sexual power given
   to you by God? When do you catch a glimpse of
   this power?

2. How do you feel about being a woman who by her
   very essence has this sort of power?

3. When Bruce Springsteen wrote about a woman's
   "secret garden," he was describing the deep essence
   of a woman that is so inviting to a man. What do
   you want a man to take the time to get to know
   about you?

4. What evidence do you find for the value that God
   places on the feminine—on the essence of being
   created a woman, not a man? What draws you
   about this? What scares you?

5. That God allows a man's sexual vulnerability to be
   subject to your permission, your reception of him,
   is a huge thing. How does this change your view of
   sexual relationships? How does it motivate you to
   be more responsible in your sexuality?

4

Power and Seduction

And I'm gonna make you love me. Oh yes, I will.
Yes, I will.

– The Temptations

Love that is real can always be refused.

– Philip Yancey

*I*n her mid-twenties, Chris looks back at her first real boyfriend in college and realizes the significance of that relationship. She had managed to ignore guys through high school. Her grades ... her grades— she had to keep her grades high to get into the school she wanted. Which Chris, to her credit, did.

Lars appeared in a text message in the spring of her freshmen year. He'd gone to the trouble to get her number from a friend. They started getting coffee after a chemistry class they were in together. He was the perfect antidote to her small-town, small-world background. As a military kid, he'd lived in a half dozen countries—all these places he wanted to take her! Chris began to like him, more than she was prepared to like any guy.

The parties he took her to weren't exactly what she would have picked. But a glass of wine gave her some distance from the craziness. And the wine also made it easier, before long, to sleep with Lars. She liked the guy, to be sure—but she hadn't set out to sleep with him.

She looks back on the next six months as some of the happiest times of her life. For the first time ever, she almost forgot her parents' divorce and her father's new family with another woman. Everything save Lars faded into a gray, silent background. She liked it better that way.

In the pit of her stomach, though, she knew this couldn't last. There was too much life in front of them. By the next spring, under the same budding trees and bursting azaleas, they agreed to move on. *It's just not the right time in our lives for a serious relationship*. Friends, yes, they would part as friends.

Chris kept drilling that mantra in her head over the next few months. Lars had been a decent first love. She would have other loves, surely. But the first time she saw Lars with another girl, laughing and flirting his head off, his arm gently slipping around her waist, Chris had to duck into the nearest women's bathroom. She thought she would throw up.

She couldn't escape the sense that she'd come out the loser. Young or not, she hadn't been enough of something to keep this guy. She'd been left behind before—by her dad— and she hated having those awful feelings again.

Chris looks back on her first love and the searing nature

of that experience as the thing that greased the skids and made it easier to have sex with other men after Lars. But from then on, she kept her heart out of the picture. At least she had learned that much.

In the space of a few years, Chris went from reluctant partner to aggressive female. Being with a guy sexually made her feel like an utterly desirable woman, for a little while at least. She felt like a woman in control. She needed a constant stream of male attention—but she made sure she wasn't the one left behind this time.

Only now, Chris looks back and wonders where the girl she remembers went.

THE SLIPPERY SLOPES OF SEDUCTIVENESS

Power games. How easily the world of relationships between men and women devolves in this direction. Both parties end up competing to ensure they aren't the ones who get left in the dust, feeling like a fool.

But there is a dark side to relationships when "power" is the driving force. And ultimately, the conversation leads to a rather breathtaking view of God.

God has given you a beautiful body. I know—you think there are ten things wrong with it. We all think there are ten things (at least) wrong with our bodies. But that doesn't change reality. You are eminently desirable, in ways you have probably only slowly discovered. And in this body, each of us undergoes a transformation as dramatic as a worm to a butterfly. The gangly middle school girl with braces sheds her old skin and emerges as a young woman. And guys notice.

Big-time. It is quite the rush to feel the power of being so attractive to a guy.

But if the wonder of that power gets twisted (and having your heart broken will truly wring out the wonder part), then a subtle, dark influence often invades. Sexual attraction becomes a tool a woman uses to get what she thinks she wants. Innocent wonder can morph into seductive power before you know what's happened.

Sex outside marriage has a disturbing tendency to drift in the direction of power and manipulation. There is no covenant, no transcendent meaning, no pledge of love through thick and thin. There's not enough material on which to build a basis for love and respect. And so the lead weight of it all sinks us into sheer human selfishness.

When author Kelly Cohen wrote a memoir of the men she'd bedded, she explained how a particular mirage drove her: somehow if she could establish a sexual connection, this man would be hers.

> There's no question in our minds that this is all it takes [luring a man into bed]. Men are so easy that way. If they have sex with you they can be yours. Even though this hasn't been the case in the past, I still believe it. It's written across every ad, every movie, every love song. *Sex equals ownership.*[1]

Isn't that exactly the illusion we are sold at every turn? Sex is supposed to be the path to belonging to someone deeply. Every movie says so. But as the remainder of Cohen's memoir reveals, not only did sex *not* make a man hers; she emerged in her late twenties feeling "no different than I was as a teenager."[2] She felt personally and emotionally stuck.

In a culture with such broken sexual boundaries, the path of sexual seductiveness is an easy one to follow. One night when I couldn't sleep, I opened up my email (always a mistake at 3:00 a.m., right?), and there on my screen was the story of a woman who had followed that path to a place where she was using sex for revenge. Her story is important to hear:

> I am halfway through your book. I bought it in search of reasons why I have for so many years now used sex to get men. I've been through one marriage and lots and lots of sexually driven relationships. Along the way, I got really hurt by a couple of men I loved.
>
> So I learned how to use my body for revenge. I meet a guy now, and I tell him that I'm celibate, but that's a big lie. I put off sex for a number of meetings, and then I "move in for the kill." When they start to have feelings for me, I back off big-time.
>
> I feel hollow inside. The only time I feel alive, really, is when I am experiencing the power of pulling a guy in. I can make him fall for me, and I can hurt him so much in the process. I can walk away and not feel a thing.
>
> But I'm scared, now. Will I always feel this dead inside? Will I ever be able to trust anyone again? I want to feel something other than the darkness and void of my own soul.

Sex outside marriage has a disturbing tendency to drift in the direction of power and manipulation.

We can be living this woman's story before we know it. When we learn the power of our attractiveness, we can take that power in some terrifically destructive directions. It's a temptation every woman faces. It's the dark side of the beauty we possess.

Notice how for Chris and the woman who wrote me anonymously, pain propelled them down this path. *I got really hurt by a couple of men I loved.* Slowly a quiet inner vow takes shape inside a woman. *I won't be the one who's left hurting. No way.* So she learns to use her body like a tool to get just enough of what she wants. Or as Solomon describes the seductive woman in the book of Proverbs:

> *With her many persuasions she entices him;*
> *With her flattering lips she seduces him.*
> *Suddenly he follows her*
> *As an ox goes to the slaughter …*
> *As a bird hastens to the snare,*
> *So he does not know that it will cost him his life.*[3]

The seductive use of sexual power is a strange thing. It burns both the lured and the lurer in nearly equal measures. A woman becomes as damaged as the man she seduces.

HOW GOD LOVES

Now this is where the discussion of power and love gets really interesting.

If you think about your close friends, you know you wouldn't even have a friendship based on power. It wouldn't survive. Manipulation usually kills even the simplest of human relationships. When it comes to love between a man and a woman, power and manipulation prove to be the kiss of death. Unless there's freedom, there's no trust. Without trust and freedom, you will never know love.

These are the laws of the relational universe, and we didn't invent them. This is the way God loves us. He loves at great cost, and he doesn't force our hand. *Love that is real can always be refused.*[4]

God turns power in relationships upside down. The One who created the world, who is the King of all kings, lays aside his power and comes to us in the utter vulnerability of a baby—and ultimately, in a cruel death on a cross. He lays aside his power in order to love.

Someone once said that if you told God's story as a parable, it would sound like this.[5]

A king came to a village and fell in love with a maiden there. His dilemma was how to win her love. He knew that he could come with his banners flying and his army at his side. He could swoop her up on the back of his horse and carry her away. He had the power to do that in a matter of moments. *But power does not win love.* And the king was wise enough to know this. So what does the king do? He puts on the clothes of a beggar and comes to live in her village in order to win her love.

The King has come to *your* village, disguised as a beggar, so that he can capture your heart with his love. That is the gospel. This story about the king is a close human analogy for what God has actually done in Jesus. It is the story the Bible tells: "And the Word became flesh, and dwelt among us, and we saw His glory … full of grace and truth."[6]

Rob Bell writes, "The story the Bible tells is of a living being who loves and who continues to love even when that love is not returned. A God who refuses to override our free-dom, who respects our power to decide whether to reciprocate, a God who lets us make the next move."[7]

> *Sex outside its intended bonds is as destructive and soul tearing as it is healing and redemptive inside the bonds it's meant for.*

So if you look at the blueprint of love and relationships, you find this same dynamic in place: the harder you try to manipulate love, the more it eludes you.

When we love someone, we actually give them the power in the relationship. We hand them a piece of our heart, taking the risk they may not want us back. We surrender the desire to control the other person's response. Only if we do that do we have even a fighting chance at love.

Human love must follow the blueprint of God's love in the surrender of power and the willingness to sacrifice your-self for another, or it ends up an aborted mess. It never looks and feels like love.

THE CURE FOR THE SEDUCTIVE HEART

The woman whose email kept me awake resorted to using her body as a way to punish men because she had given up the hope that she might actually be loved by one.

The temptation to seduce a man in order to feel loved or powerful can only be cured by a greater love.

If who I am as a woman is truly grounded in being loved by God, then I am free to love in a radically new way.

The relational world opens up before me with a host of possibilities.

It's OK if you don't love me. I can handle it if you don't want me ... like me ... need me. It's really OK.

I am an outrageously loved woman.

You are this woman whom Jesus loves. The freedom that comes from this awareness makes real love at the right time with the right man such a beautiful possibility. It deserves a white dress and a roomful of flowers; truly it does. Oh, the healing nature of a sexual relationship with the man you marry, having checked the power games at the door, not searching for love and meaning in your life but able to offer yourself out of this deep well of being a woman already loved!

Then all the power that God has placed in sexual love is yours to the max. Rob Bell writes:

> But sex is not the search for something that's missing. It's the expression of something that's been found. It's designed to be the overflow, the culmination of something that a man and a woman have found in each other. It's a celebration of this living, breathing thing that's happening between the two of them.[8]

Let me close with a story that gives a picture of the healing that is possible in the goodness of love.

Tess always wondered if there was a man out there who could handle her size. She was the daughter of a basketball coach, Amazonian in size. Her personality was as large as her person; she filled up a room with conversation and laughter.

Tess dated a lot of men. But what might have been romance always turned into friendship. She was every guy's best girl friend, but she was not the woman they fell in love with.

You could trace part of the problem to an awful moment in high school when she was at her heaviest. Her father was known in the community for being a great basketball coach; his children knew him for his drinking. One night he was going to take Tess to help him scout an opposing team's defense, but he'd had "a few too many." When Tess came down the stairs, he took one look at her and said, "I'm not taking you to a basketball game. I'm ashamed to be seen with you."

For Tess, no apology the next day could undo the damage. The last thing she wanted was to be some man's embarrassment.

So from that point in her life, whenever she hung out with a guy, she made sure she walked three or four paces ahead. Give him a little breathing room—he won't want anyone to think we're together. It wasn't the easiest way to carry on a conversation, but Tess managed.

The summer she turned thirty, she met a guy at a youth camp where they were both counselors between regular teaching jobs. He was a few years younger but just as tall. By the end of June, he was finding excuses to help her with her campers. Finally, he asked her out to dinner.

Tess did her usual thing. She got out of the car and started walking fast. But this man ran to catch up with her. Joe put his hand on the small of her back and walked alongside. Tess says that this small gesture changed her life. It was the first time she felt attractive to a man—and worth something. He wasn't ashamed of her.

Twenty years and three children later, she can still feel the significance of his touch.[9]

This is just the tiniest picture of how God uses the power of our sexuality not to destroy or undo but to bring healing and a love that lasts.

Questions for Discussion and Reflection

1. What kind of power games in relationships have you observed or experienced, and how do sexual experiences complicate this tendency?

2. Where do you draw the line between enjoying your attractiveness to a guy and using it inappropriately?

3. How does power backfire in relationships? Have you ever experienced a power struggle? How did it affect the relationship?

4. Does the realization that God deeply loves you change your view of relationships with men? How?

5. What attracts you—what draws your heart—about the way God loves?

5

Protective Fences

Our mothers pined for liberation, and we are pining for interference.

– WENDY SHALIT

People always say, "She's such a pretty girl—she must have loads of boyfriends." Sometime I think I sleep with men to prove I'm attractive, I'm normal. I have sex so people won't think there's something wrong with me.

– AMY, AGE ٢٢

A quiet stroll through a shopping mall, looking not for an item to purchase but how such items are marketed, can be a major eye-opening experience. Especially when it comes to women's clothing.

This fact struck me recently as I walked by the front of a store that sells brand-name jeans. There in the window is a larger-than-life beautiful couple, halfway to naked. The picture practically pulsates. If the billboard were a video clip, in about thirty seconds this couple would be in bed. I find myself looking around and wondering if anyone else sees this.

So I do the obvious thing—or at least it seems obvious to me. I walk in and ask for the manager, a savvy, overly stressed woman hardly thirty-five years old.

"Tell me about your billboard," I say, with as neutral a voice as I can muster. And then with a little more punch, I add, "How can you bear to sell your jeans this way?"

The manager is surprised, but I can tell she's been asked this question before. She's a polite professional. "Oh, you know, we have no control over what they send us from New York."

This is a peek into a much larger story—and one that affects you and me more than we can imagine. Sexy sells. In fact, it sells so well that even Disney has discovered that dolling up their princess line for three-year-olds increases their sales volume noticeably. Educational psychologists Diane Levin and Jean Kilbourne write in their book *So Sexy So Soon*: "Marketers have long targeted children as potential consumers and they know that using sex and sexiness is one of the most successful ways to get children's attention in order to make them want to shop."[1]

Now I could digress into pointing out how women are being manipulated into buying something that will make them feel wanted by a man. Our vulnerability is exploited to line someone else's pocket. But that's not exactly my point. It's only an important step to where I'm going.

My real question for you to ponder is what does it mean to grow up in a culture where so many protective fences have been torn down—where there aren't fathers and front parlors and selective filters that would have allowed you to be a girl whose innocence really, really, mattered?

This question comes stumbling into a counseling office like mine, usually voiced by a woman in her early- to mid-twenties. She comes wondering why she feels hollow, empty, and unable to risk much in any close relationship. All these guys line up in her head—the ones she loved, the total jerks, the ones whose names she can't remember.

> *"Why didn't I hear more about the cost of living as if sex had no consequences, no meaning?*

She has begun to think about her life. Why, she asks, didn't my parents put up a bigger fuss when they knew I was having sex with that guy in high school? Why did I listen to "friends" who acted like being a virgin was a plague to be rid of?

Or as one woman poignantly put it, "Why didn't I hear more about the cost of living as if sex had no consequences, no meaning? *Where was everybody?*"

FEELING THE ABSENCE OF BOUNDARIES

When you think of your own life, who were the people who went out of their way to talk with you about sexuality? We all know it's a bit of an awkward conversation. But who swallowed the awkwardness and told you that you were worth waiting for, worth the lifelong pledge of some man's love?

Who got in your face, maybe with tears in their eyes, when they discovered you weren't listening? How would someone who cared have gotten past your anger in order to love you into thinking about where this path would take you?

Did anyone tell you that God made you for more?

If there's been little or no dialogue, it can leave a girl feeling like she's on her own. She concludes she's not worth much fuss. And the pressure is so great out there, it screams in your face.

Many of us have stories similar to that of my friend Heather. She's quite the attractive woman now, but she swears if you had met her when she was thirteen, you'd have seen a gawky, pimply faced, shy teenager. She turned no heads. And because her family moved a lot, she never stayed in any one place long enough to make real friends. She saw herself as the girl-left-out.

But then her body began taking shape and her pimple problem was cured by a good dermatologist. Guys began to notice her for the first time. Oh, how good it felt to be noticed! She can feel the initial rush to this day. The more she played on her assets, the more of an insider she became.

It was like following a recipe she never admitted to herself she was following: *Give this guy a little of the sexual stuff he wants — and I will feel a little less alone.* Following this pattern made having sex with a guy just an obvious step in a progression she had no idea how to stop. It became the way she operated with guys — more guys than she could count. A few moments of feeling really wanted — in exchange for sexual intimacy. Eventually, while she looked like a sharp, professional woman, inside she felt like a prostitute with a briefcase.

For Heather, one of the best parts of turning to Christ

was that he gave her a new ability to put up boundaries in her own heart—to say no for reasons that made sense.

"Would you have listened to someone when you were sixteen?" I ask her.

Heather is not sure. Maybe she would have blown them off. But she so wishes she'd had more friends and family challenging her to guard her sexuality.

WHY BOUNDARIES MATTER

All this begs the issue of what boundaries in our lives are meant to do.

Think of the most basic sexual boundary we know. A parent does not have sex with or make sexual overtures toward his child. That's called incest. It's an instinctual taboo in every culture that survives. But why? Why draw lines anywhere if the guiding light is merely satisfying a physical or emotional desire on someone's part? *Why not?*

Thinking about boundaries really has to start at a primal place because we are living in primal places with each other these days. Any time we reduce something with transcendent meaning (a sexual experience) into an exchange of pleasure, we are stepping backward.

Simply put, boundaries convey value. Of all things expected of a man (or a parent), protecting the innocence and purity of a wife or son or daughter or sister is right at the top of the list. Do you remember the hairy Scottish father in the movie *Braveheart*? William Wallace had to get past this father as he stood at the door of his family hut in the pouring rain in order to even think of riding off with his daughter for an afternoon.

So, unfortunately, if we've grown up with few boundaries put in place in the way we relate to men, we often conclude we aren't worth much.

Boundaries mark something or someone as special, set apart, worth going to a lot of trouble for. The kinds of practices that protect have a long and colorful history. Ancient Jewish law, for example, corralled the sexual experience to the bonds of marriage between one man and one woman for a lifetime, and then it celebrated the place of sex. Even the government could not conscript a man for war during his first year of marriage, because bringing pleasure to his wife was literally his job description: "If a man has recently married, he must not be sent to war or have any other duty laid on him. For one year he is to be free to stay at home and bring happiness to the wife he has married."[2]

Without trust, nothing lasting is built in a relationship.

God, then, as the ultimate Father, draws boundaries around the experience of sexual intimacy so that it becomes a huge yes inside the protected relationship of marriage. You have only to read with open eyes the Song of Songs to realize just how hugely sex is celebrated in marriage. One huge screaming yes!

In Jewish culture, you find an old saying that speaks volumes: "The daughters of Israel are not available for public use." Their lack of sexual availability stems from their high value. Putting a fence around sexual expression is a way of saying you are special. Your innocence and purity belong to you alone. They are part of the giving of yourself to a man—an amazing gift. A healthy society will protect your sexual innocence, not exploit it in the rush for a larger profit margin.

Boundaries also play a huge role in the deepening of a relationship with a man you might even want to spend your life enjoying. A kind of exquisite tension develops as a romance takes off. You are forced, in all the best ways, to push out the borders of your relationship. You have a special span of time to stockpile the building materials of a relationship that can last—the sense of being enjoyed by another, respect, and especially trust. Without trust, nothing lasting is built in a relationship. Allowing for a period of life devoted to courtship without fanning the flames of sex is the best gift two people in love could claim for themselves. It is the heart of romance.

But once sex enters the scene, it dominates the whole picture for a while—and rightly so. Sex was meant to be consuming. That's what honeymoons are for: giving couples time for the celebration of sex. And that's why people with good memories leave a couple alone for a fair number of months after they are married.

On a practical level, then, there are at least three huge reasons boundaries in sexuality lead to more rather than less.

1. Boundaries give your relationship the chance to grow in all the important, foundational ways that make for something lasting.
2. Boundaries convey worth and value to your sexuality; they protect your soul.
3. Healthy sexual boundaries protect the emotional space around the experience of sex in marriage.

MAKING SENSE OF THE PAIN

The sad irony, of course, is that women have clamored for total sexual freedom—for the absence of boundaries. And while it's good that the female experience of sexual pleasure is validated now and a woman isn't solely defined by her attachment to a man, most women feel something vital is missing.

Women often look back on losing their virginity and wish more had been made of the significance of their innocence—as though it could only be seen in the rearview mirror after it had been lost. Thousands of girls identify with Naomi Wolf, whose book *The Beauty Myth* exposed the way our culture's demand for "beauty" exploits women. Wolf writes about the day she and her high school boyfriend made an appointment at a local health clinic so she could get fitted for a diaphragm and they could have sex. She says the experience was like a trip to a vet; she felt processed on an animal level. "It was easier than getting your learner's permit to drive a car," she writes.[3]

She goes on to say that her experience of sex itself was a trifle disappointing—not awful, certainly not good. It was what it was. She remembers kissing her boyfriend good-bye and going home to think about what had happened—and then getting angry. "That's it?" she said to herself. "That's all my virginity is worth?" In a culture that denies the meaning of sex, that's where it ends up—mechanistic, trivial, demeaning.

The tip-off that sex is far more than a physical act lies in the anger and disappointment and loss this woman felt. It is this pain that tells us we are human beings, created in the image of God, with souls capable of crying out.

You can see the spiral downward articulated clearly in a recent novel, *College Girl*. Patricia Weitz writes about how Natalie Bloom found her way from an impoverished background into an elite university by sheer, determined hard work. She hung out in the library, a shy, bookish girl hoping no one would discover how insecure she felt.

But Patrick, this classy guy from a privileged family, started hanging out with her.

"I like you," he said. He seemed so totally at ease with her social bumblings. She had sex with him because she sensed that while "a priest could wipe away sin," being with Patrick could wipe away insecurity in ways that earning A's never could. How did she feel, though, in this first sexual experience that set her up for many others?

> I was no longer a virgin. *No longer a virgin*. It was too soon to know exactly how I felt, but I didn't feel good. I didn't feel like a "woman." Most important, I didn't feel loved or ... saved. I closed my eyes and recalled the one thing about sex that I *had* enjoyed: I hadn't been able to think about anything. No worries, no thought, no self-conscious anxiety. That had been nice. But afterwards, *instantaneously*, the thoughts were back, full force, and all of them were telling me to feel disappointed.[4]

LONGING FOR LIMITS

Reading a novel like *College Girl*, in which the author describes a young woman's years-long search for limits and her struggle as a woman who deserved to be loved to find a relationship with a man, helps me realize how long and arduous this process of forming boundaries where you never had any can be.

Let me suggest that while a search for boundaries is necessary, the source of healthy boundaries is God. It's actually quite difficult to come up with boundaries that make much sense apart from God! (As in, you really, really have to work at this task).

But if your beginning place is actually the Beginning, you find the road is paved and the scenery is breathtaking. I didn't write this book to make you feel bad about your past. No, a thousand times no. I wrote this to describe the relational possibilities that come with a clean heart and a fresh start. I know it's like learning the alphabet again, but that's OK. This alphabet predates you; it's been around since the dawn of time.

A God who loves you gave you a body, and that body has meaning. What you do with that body matters. It's out of this meaning that boundaries come.

That's why it really bothers me when someone tries to shove jeans down our throats by making us believe we'll be totally sexy inside them. And I mourn the loss of strong fathers and front parlors. But these sad realities, as well as the sexualizing of an entire culture, means that the protective fences around sex must now be inside our own heads. The boundaries must be internalized.

As you read this book, you may be taking your own steps to establish or reclaim an inner sense of sexual boundaries. Sometimes we don't even know we've crossed a boundary until we go back and see what we stumbled over.

In the upcoming chapters, you'll see more clearly how these boundaries are derived from the meaning behind sexual experience—a meaning that reflects the very nature of God and his love for you.

Discovering the beauty and meaning behind sex is to reclaim the integrity of your own soul as well. For women who lost their virginity somewhere along the way, it's like taking back ground lost in a war. You see something rich and meaningful and entirely possible on the horizon—a relationship with a man that is unfettered and nourishing, without the sexual baggage of having slept together.

A God who loves you gave you a body, and that body has meaning. What you do with that body matters.

If there is anything good about living in a culture that sells sex by the yard, it's the fact that sexual boundaries cannot easily be imposed from outside. They have to be claimed—or reclaimed—from within, where the only real boundaries are formed. They are not forced on you by parents or college handbooks or cultural norms.

Real boundaries are those you embrace for yourself.

Questions for Discussion and Reflection

1. If our mothers threw off restraints and today's women "are pining for interference," as Wendy Shalit claims, in what ways do you see women wanting to be interfered with—wanting someone to encourage their sexual integrity?

2. What kind of protective fences have there been for you with regard to your sexuality? How did you feel about those influences at the time? Now?

3. Where do you wish more effort had been made to protect your sexuality?

4. In the absence of sexual boundaries, how do you see women actually becoming weaker and more vulnerable?

5. What kind of process or choices would you need in order to live with a sense of sexual boundaries that come from your inner being? Do these boundaries seem like deprivation, or freedom and choice?

6

Stepping on Each Other's Toes

We all need a little tenderness. How can love survive in such a graceless age?

—"THE HEART OF THE MATTER,"
lyrics by Don Henley, Mike Campbell, and J. D. Souther

Carelessly, thoughtlessly, casually, sex—in the short space of a single generation—went from being the culminating act of committed love to being a precondition, a tryout, for future involvement. If any.

—DANIELLE CRITTENDEN

When a man and woman fall in love, it's a delicate, breathtakingly beautiful dance. In any generation, it's a high-stakes tango. Two people leave separate existences and walk into an unknown future because they believe it will be better together. And for a woman, as much as we may pretend otherwise, the secret longing of our hearts is for a man to really put himself out there. It used to be called "courting." No one would dare use that word now. But the longing is the same: to be wooed and won as a woman whose heart is worth going to a bit of trouble for.

Let me say it as clearly as I know how: You are made to be wooed and won—courted, if you please—by a guy who sees the uniqueness of who you are. This is the heart of romance. And it mirrors the great Romance of the ages—of a God who turned the world upside down to capture our love and to bring us to our true home in him.

I saw the beauty of a good relationship play out recently in our son's life. If you knew Brady, he would tell you quickly that he's made mistakes with women. But he learned from them. He especially learned the importance of prayer. As he prayed, he began to get to know a woman named Hannah (they were both counselors at a youth camp one summer). At that point in her life, Hannah felt there was such a dearth of eligible men that if God wanted to bring a suitable one her way, "he'd have to drop him right out of the sky." Actually, that's exactly what God did. Brady is a pilot.

When it became clear over a number of months that the relationship was heading toward marriage, Brady began to plan the best way to surprise Hannah with a ring. One morning, he called her and asked if he could pick her up and get a bagel. Only they drove past the exit and kept going—out into the country to the place where a friend with a private plane kept his hangar. Brady flew Hannah to the Outer Banks of North Carolina and proposed to her on the beach. When they flew back to Raleigh, both sets of parents met them at the airport, and we all went out to dinner.

Hardly ever in my life have I been in a setting in which I could so distinctly feel the joy of God—the utter joy of God as he brings a man and a woman together. Oh, it can be such a beautiful dance!

THE LONGING FOR BEAUTY

Even in this age of playing everything cool, the human longing to experience the beauty of relationship still shows up in full force. It sneaks out when we aren't looking. When I'm teaching a group seminar on this subject, I often show a clip from the timeless movie *Braveheart*. Something about Mel Gibson speaking in Scottish brogue seems to strip away pretense. It's the story of the ages, told all over again. Here is one man and one woman looking for the love of their lives and for a cause that matters. Some things never change.

Follow me into one unforgettable scene. William Wallace comes calling for Murron, a young woman to whom he has been attracted for some time. The family banters back and forth until suddenly Murron leaps onto the back of William's horse and together they ride bareback across the vast glen. They spend the afternoon getting to know each other. He tells her all the places he has been, worlds away from Scotland. He speaks in French about how lovely he finds her. She is suitably wowed. The birth of this love closes with a scene of the two of them sitting atop a cliff watching the sun set in the distance.

This is a love William is willing to risk everything for. And indeed, Murron's death at the hands of the king's soldiers is the catalyst that incites him to war against England for the freedom of Scotland.

When I show this film clip, it is almost always followed by complete silence. For a few moments, a deep, ageless place in each of us opens up. Our cynical aloofness is stripped away to expose the raw, aching longing for the kind of beauty that is possible only between a man and a woman.

You can see this beauty captured on occasion at a wedding. Against a backdrop in which everyone present knows the couple will face their own measure of heartache and trouble ahead, each pledges love and commitment to the other in the face of the great unknown. The courage required, if you really think about it, is staggering. The beauty of the event is a borrowed one, on loan from the story of the ages that will end at a wedding and lavish feast. The Bridegroom awaits even now. The bride is making herself ready for the day when the Bridegroom has promised to present her to himself "without stain or wrinkle or any other blemish."[1]

When the soil of your heart is primed to receive love, this courting dance is a clean and beautiful thing.

There is a simple, timeless beauty to this courting dance itself: discovering someone you click with, having him go out of his way to be with you, feeling completely at home together, and experiencing an odd, inconsolable ache when he is away. When the soil of your heart is primed to receive love, this courting dance is a clean and beautiful thing. Every generation recognizes this beauty and bows its head in wonder. Even the book of Proverbs, that ancient source of wisdom, comments on the dance:

There are three things that are too amazing for me,
   four that I do not understand:
the way of an eagle in the sky,
   the way of a snake on a rock,
the way of a ship on the high seas,
   and the way of a man with a maiden.[2]

I should mention that the word *amazing* is literally the word *beautiful* in Hebrew. So the height of beauty and sheer, inscrutable mystery is the way an eagle soars in the sky or a ship sails on a bright, blue sea—or a man and woman fall in love.

If you and I were not tuned to want the beauty of a good relationship, we would not be appalled when things turn cheap and ugly. Somehow we know a relationship is not meant to degenerate into abandonment or jealous rage. There is nothing beautiful about a broken heart. The relationship should work out—or the two parties part in a decent peace.

I suggest that we consider the strange and macabre role that sex plays in all that pain. When the potential for goodness and beauty is so great, how then does sex usher in its own sort of ugly? How does the dance end in bloodied toes?

EXPECTING TOO LITTLE FROM A MAN

One way in which the beauty of the dance is being lost is that allowing sex to be part of a dating relationship invites men to be their worst selves. Indeed, it is a common complaint among women—men seem to be more boorish, as though they have a right to expect sexual favors.

When journalist Laura Sessions Stepp conducted dozens of interviews with girls whose introduction to sex was a series of "hooking up" experiences, she concluded that "without having previously experienced the thoughtfulness of decent boyfriends, many girls, sadly, have no idea what they should expect."[3]

Do you remember Lou Bega's hit song a few years back? In a catchy little mambo tune, he sang about wanting a little bit of Sandra—all night long. And a little bit of Mary. And oh, while he was at it, a little bit of Jessica. And for these little bits of women, he was gallantly willing to be "their man." Their man for a moment, while he was getting his "little bit." How did we ever, ever convince ourselves that this was normal?

The really sad part is that when we expect too little from a man—when we let him get by with his "boorish self"—we disrespect him. He is capable of so much more. And he knows this. Men rise to the level of women's expectations. They always have. So when we see them as sexual objects and when we permit them to treat us as sexual objects, we both become something less human.

When was the last time a guy went out of his way to do a thoughtful thing for you? If he attempts to open a door for you, do you feel appreciated and valued—or do you feel you're too weak to open the door for yourself? Maybe it would be wise to just stand there and see. *Can I let myself look for thoughtful, considerate behavior from a guy and take the risk he might not do a thing?* Trust me—he will in time. As we'll see in the last chapter, a man is put on the planet with the responsibility to look beyond his own self-interest and to care for others. But if we women don't grasp this reality, then often—quite often—he won't either.

Allowing a relationship to turn sexual sends a signal that men read clearly: You don't have to be responsible.

In the great androgynous experiment we have lived through, where it seems weak to expect a man to treat you differently because you are a woman, we have raised a generation of men who are trained to think that women are just like them. To give us special treatment would imply that we are needy in ways that men are not. We cannot be too surprised at men's boorish behavior. If sex is what they want from a relationship, they assume this is what a woman wants, too. "No" has historically been seen as a woman's rightful prerogative. But in today's sexual climate, "no" is interpreted by many men as a personal rebuke to something they thought they had a right to expect.

"Men *are* getting away with appalling behavior toward women. But we are letting them get away with it—and then … refusing to admit it to ourselves," writes social commentator Danielle Crittenden.[4] Allowing a relationship to turn sexual sends a signal that men read clearly: *You don't have to be responsible.* It tells a guy that very little is expected of him, and sure enough, he conforms to this expectation. It is no compliment to a man, however. He knows he is getting away with something. And part of him realizes that he does not deserve your respect, which in the male psyche is the validation he most truly craves.

Sexual license in a relationship tends to cancel out customary graces, as though telling the truth even when it's hard or other such selfless acts are small, unimportant courtesies. It makes the whole dance more about what I'm getting than what I'm giving, and this is the beginning of the end in any relationship. Promiscuity is, by definition, a "taking" event, a loud way of saying, "I will have my needs met," and as such, it paves the way for our worst character to emerge.

Have you noticed that in some crucial way a man wants you to expect the world from him? He sees in the mirror of your expectations someone who believes the best about him. And if you see him as a guy worthy of respect, able to look out for you and other people, someone who has his head together, then he believes it a little more of himself. You do him no favor when you expect too little. Wendy Shalit writes, "Too many egalitarians equate male gentleness or protectiveness with subordination, while too many conservatives equate it with effeminacy. Both sides are wrong. A man should be gentle around a woman. That's part of what it means to be a man."[5]

SEX IN A RELATIONSHIP YOU HOPE IS FOR KEEPS

Always the question emerges: Isn't sex in a committed relationship a little less injurious? Even more, is it not totally understandable when it happens between a couple who have an "understanding" of sorts that marriage is in the offing? Is not the beauty of the relationship preserved?

This is a hard question to answer. If you compare it to building a house, it is like hoping the house can be built successfully, even though something is chipping away at the foundation as you build. It can be done. Good houses are constructed under duress. But who would willingly want to take those risks with the central human relationship of their lives?

The major building block of a close and intimate relationship is trust. Marriage vows are the equivalent of looking someone straight in the eye and saying, "As much as I am able, I trust you above all others with my life." Sex before marriage eats away at this very trust. Always the nagging question hangs in the background: How would you feel about me if sex weren't in this picture? Do you love me for me?

Couples who have sex before marriage find that jealousy and mistrust creep in more easily on the far side of the honeymoon. They know a boundary has been crossed in the past. Since neither had the strength of will and character to prevent sexual intimacy between them, what's to keep from crossing a sexual boundary again, only this time with someone else?

Especially with regard to marriage, sex clouds the issue at hand. It's so hard to think straight! I hear many men and women admit after marriage that they did not really know the person they married—not really. Sex filled in the spaces. After a while they weren't sure if the attachment was to the person or the sex. Everything got blurred. Combining sex with a serious relationship among two people not yet married is a bit like going to an art auction drunk, where you're intending to spend your life savings. If ever you needed to make a decision with your head, marriage is it. *Who is this man? What is his heart really like?*

DEVALUING YOURSELF AS A WOMAN

One rainy fall day, a woman came to my office and told me how tired she was of the whole relationship scene. What she meant was that she had gone from one relationship to the next for the last six years, and she despaired of ever finding a guy she would want to bring home to her parents.

"I'm seeing a man right now who seems almost too good to be true," she said a little wistfully. "It's only been a couple of months, but I'm just waiting for him to stop calling or to take up with someone else."

"Are you telling me you see some red flags in this guy?" I asked, thinking maybe he wasn't as good as he looked.

"No," she said quickly. "It's not him. It's me. I'm waiting for him to find something about me he doesn't like. There must be something I'm missing."

This is how our sexual past can screw up a perfectly good relationship in the present. These men who have come and gone twist our minds out of shape. We believe lies about ourselves: I don't deserve to be loved. I have some hidden flaw that will mess everything up. When this man discovers I'm not perfect, he'll leave—just like they always do.

This is where the dance between men and women loses nearly all of its beauty. This kind of self-devaluation becomes a self-fulfilling prophecy. How you see yourself becomes the way you invite others to see you.

Truthfully, I know of no way out of this dark place in the forest other than turning to a love that is bigger and deeper than any man's—the cleansing, restoring love of Christ. You can try every self-help remedy out there, but none of them get to the source of the pain—the shame of seeing yourself as less than lovable.

I often am drawn back to a story in the gospel of John of a woman who knew more shame and rejection than most of us will encounter in a lifetime.[6] Picture this scene. It is early morning; the sun is just beginning to warm the stones beneath bare feet. Jesus is preparing to teach in the temple courts, but a loud commotion interrupts him. A woman, half naked, shamed out of her skin, is dragged before Jesus by a group of men who want to stone her to death, as the law allows. Her sin? Having been caught in the act of adultery. (One wonders where the man went.)

No one rises to the woman's defense. She makes no plea, no attempt to escape. She has no advocate. She is stripped of honor and any sense of worth. Those who are dragging her before Jesus are not really concerned about her adultery and certainly are not concerned about her. Their only goal is to trap Jesus. Will Jesus uphold the law that permits her stoning? How will he deal with a guilty woman?

Jesus does not answer her accusers at first. He stoops down and writes in the dirt something mysterious and unrecorded in the text. Then he issues a challenge that turns everything on its heels. "Let any one of you who is without sin be the first to throw a stone at her,"[7] he says, and one by one, beginning with the oldest, the men walk away until Jesus is alone with this woman.

She could run away easily now and hide in the shadows of her shame. But she chooses to stay with the one person who could justifiably cast a stone. She is in no hurry to leave. Perhaps this is the first time in her life she has felt entirely safe in a man's company. Jesus straightens up and looks into her eyes. This moment is just between the two of them.

"Woman, where are they? Has no one condemned you?"

"No one, sir," she said.

"Then neither do I condemn you. Go now and leave your life of sin."[8]

A close friend who for years has coached people through significant life change says that people never really change very deeply until someone catches them in their shame and is not appalled. That's exactly what happened in this story. Jesus caught this woman in the place where everyone else would throw her away—the place of her sin and shame. Yet he takes her by the hand and leads her to freedom.

This story holds the secret to how any of us discovers the love of God in the places in our souls we would most want to hide. Jesus sees, as no one ever has, the broken, sinful places in us where we have sought every other love but his—where we feel like a prostitute, where we think of ourselves as undeserving of love, where we know that no one who saw us this way would want us.

Jesus does not turn away. He steps right into the mess we have made and offers us not another stone of condemnation but, of all things, mercy. Without minimizing in the slightest what we have done, he offers us mercy. We can go home now. In fact, he is the home we go to, and he gives us the power to live a vastly different life. Out of this place where we have been loved in our shame, we come to know ourselves as women worthy of love. And this love changes everything.

Knowing yourself as a woman worthy of love is a very different place from which to relate to a man. The secret of most relationships is that others follow our cues. If we have no respect for ourselves, we invite others' disrespect. And if we have been embraced by a love as vast and powerful as the love of Jesus, we will know what to hope for from a man. We will not be willing to take the crumbs from under the table of love.

BETTING THE FARM

Whatever would mark the dance between men and women is meant to be beautiful. This beauty is built on courage. If there is no real investment in a relationship—no active renunciation of all others, no willingness to sacrifice my interests for yours—the whole affair starts to smell. It quickly wilts and withers. Passion is made of sturdier things, and the foremost among them is courage. Unless we are truly brave hearts, we cannot waltz with a man in a dance worth dancing.

What no one ever actually says out loud is that this delicate, beautiful dance between a man and a woman leads to a cliff. There, dressed in their finest, before an assembled crowd of friends and family, they hold hands and jump together into thin air. *For better or for worse, in sickness and in health, forsaking all others—parted only by death.* They promise to love each other in their unlovable moments and to offer respect in times when there is not a heaping lot to admire. They literally bet the farm. It is right that they do so, because beauty requires this kind of courage. Always.

Author Frederick Buechner writes:

> They say they will love, comfort, honor each other to the end of their days. They say they will cherish each other and be faithful to each other always. They say they will do these things not just when they feel like it but even … when they don't feel like it at all. In other words, the vows they make at a marriage could hardly be more extravagant.[9]

Courage comes in many forms. For many, it takes shape by degrees. I think of a woman, for instance, who felt she needed to make a sharp break in the way she had been relating to men. She felt God was leading her into a place of deeper vulnerability as a woman—the vulnerability of *not* sharing a sexual relationship with the guys she dated. In the past, it had been easier to relate physically to guys—sex kept them happy, and she felt temporarily secure. To check sex at the door and offer a man just "me, myself, and I," required far more guts. Gone was her old sense of feeling in control. Real vulnerability always translates into courage.

Real vulnerability always translates into courage.

Moreover, it takes courage to let your sexual life go dormant once it has been up and running. Sex is the convergence of many sensations, an incomparable experience. But when sexual desire is awakened before its time, "desire becomes lust, and lust is restless and shrouded in shame," as Lisa

Bevere states.[10] Eventually the experience itself is spoiled. If you've been "awakened" to sex, then you know that allowing this part of your life to rest, to go dormant, brings questions of real trust and courage: If I let this go, will I experience it again? Will God resurrect the experience of sexual intimacy with the man I marry in a way that will make all I've known seem like a faded postcard from a place I was never meant to visit?

And finally, if you have felt burned in your relationships with men, it takes courage to let yourself hope—or hope again—for all the good a man has to give. The makings of romance are hidden in this hunger for the kind of strength and solidity that men bring to your life—something uniquely and wonderfully male that cannot be replicated in friendships with other women. To cup your hands around this flame and protect it from the winds of disappointment until the right man comes along is no small thing; it is an enormous act of courage.

This kind of inner waiting—this willingness to hope—is right at the heart of being a woman who is preparing to enter the dance of her life.

Questions for Discussion and Reflection

1. When do you catch a glimpse of the beauty that is possible between a man and a woman?

2. How do you sense that sex raises the stakes in a relationship?

3. What would it mean in your life to expect more in your relationships with men?

4. Think about the woman who was dragged to Jesus by a mob intent on stoning her for adultery. What stands out in the way Jesus treated her? What in this account draws you to Jesus?

5. What shape of expression of courage is most needed in your relationships with men?

7

What Really Happens in Sex

There is no union on earth like the consummation of the love between a man and a woman. No other connection reaches as deeply as this oneness was meant to; no other passion is nearly so intense. People don't jump off bridges because they lost a grandparent. If their friend makes another friend, they don't shoot them both.... Troy didn't go down in flames because somebody lost a pet. The passion that spousal love evokes is instinctive, irrational, intense, and dare I say it, immortal.

– JOHN ELDREDGE

The smell of roses gently nudged her out of a deep sleep. Tiny shafts of bright sunlight peered around the curtains beside her bed, and for a minute she struggled to recall where she was. She was slowly being stirred awake. This morning was different from any other she had known, for one noticeable reason. Lying beside her was a man.

It came back to her in a flood of jumbled images—a wedding and a bad case of nerves, the blur of friends' faces at their small reception, her mother's tears as she left with this man who was now her husband, the flowers in their hotel room. Thinking of the shy awkwardness of their intimacy made her smile. Sex had been nothing spectacular in and of itself. It was a long way from Hollywood to be sure, yet it had been an experience so personal, so deeply altering, that it felt like she had woken up on another planet.

She lay her head on her husband's chest, watching the rise and fall, the steady rhythm of his breathing. His arm pulled her closer. She had known him for a couple of years now, yet overnight so much had changed between them. It surprised her how different she felt because of the intimacy she had shared with this man. Something in her had been touched on a level she hardly knew existed. She belonged to someone in a way she never had before. Maybe this is what it's like to feel married, she thought.

~✦

Waking up the morning after is one of those truly private moments in life when neither your thoughts nor your experience should be up for public display. It belongs to you alone. I write about it, though, as a way of issuing an invitation to explore the mystery of how a man and woman are bonded on a deep level, where trust and naked honesty lay them bare before each other in the experience of sexual intimacy. A bond like no other is begun in this place. If ever there was a human encounter in which more happens than meets the eye, it's sex.

Hearing women talk about their lives has afforded me a kind of window I never thought I'd have into the mystery of it all. All the therapy on the planet cannot accomplish what the arms of the man you love can.

In counseling you hear a woman talk about the way sexual abuse as a child ravaged her sense of herself. Or a woman might explain how being adopted made her question just how lovable she was. Or perhaps a woman realizes how the loss of her father left her grasping for attention or approval. She might share a wound like this as though it's partially healed, something she has begun to move past.

So I would ask, of course, how has this ache in her subsided?

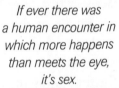

If ever there was a human encounter in which more happens than meets the eye, it's sex.

You can't imagine how often a woman will admit that the safety and security she experiences in the physical love of her husband has been a significant healing place for her.

She is saying that in the recurrent sexual drama of being held in all her vulnerability in the arms of a man who has pledged himself to her, come what may—something broken, deeper than words can touch, is being healed, piece by tiny piece.

I nod my head in understanding, realizing that words are useless in the presence of mystery.

A MYSTERIOUS BOND

Each of us carries an ache inside that seems to be met uniquely through sexual union. John Eldredge writes, "When God created Eve, as you recall, he took her straight from Adam's side. None of us has fully recovered from the surgery. There is an aloneness, an incompleteness that we experience every day of our lives. How often do you feel deeply and truly known?"[1] This deep ache to know and be known is healed at least temporarily through union with another. And from this experience a bond like no other on earth begins to form.

The word *sex* has a paradoxical sort of meaning, being derived from the Latin root *secare*, which means "to sever, amputate, or disconnect from the whole." So our sexuality is about our longing to reconnect and about all the various ways we reach out to others. Sex is but the most intimate form that longing takes.

Truly, a bond like no other on the planet is created through the experience of sexual intimacy. You can join a sorority or go on a rafting trip or work on a political campaign and you'll feel connected—bonded—to others. But there is no bond that compares with sex. And the reason for that is hidden right in the middle of the classic Bible verse you hear at most weddings:

> "For this reason a man shall leave his father and his mother, and be joined to his wife; and w shall become one flesh."[2]

The Hebrew word for *joined* means "to adhere." A man
and a woman leave their original families and "stick to" each
other. The glue, amazingly enough, is sex. God creates sex
as the superglue of the soul, a glue strong enough to create
a bond that lasts a lifetime. It's a frame that holds the two
of them together when the days are dark and there are no
words strong enough to make everything OK.

The bond that sex creates runs deeper than words can
express. It helps explain why a newly married couple feel they
belong to each other in a way they did not the day before their
wedding. Or as one young wife in her first few months of
marriage told me, "I've noticed that when my husband's neck
hurts, it feels like mine does too." The early stages of bonding
are just like that—you are becoming so connected to another
person that for a while you aren't sure where you stop and he
begins. Listen to the way Solomon describes the experience:

> *I have come into my garden, my sister, my bride;*
> *I have gathered my myrrh with my spice.*
> *I have eaten my honeycomb and my honey;*
> *I have drunk my wine and my milk.*

And God himself responds:

> *Eat, O friends, and drink;*
> *drink your fill, O lovers.*[3]

God knew it would take something special between a
man and a woman to bear the weight of life together. Bonding

means that when you are irritated with this man, when you hate his haircut—even when he does something terribly disappointing—you are still deeply connected. His is the first face you look for in a crowd.

Even in the physiology of sex, you can see the fingerprints of God and the intentional way he brings a man and woman together.

My daughter recently asked me a question that gets at the heart of bonding. "Mom," she said, "do you still think of Dad as a good-looking man?"

Her question caught me totally by surprise. I had to think about that one.

"Well, I know he used to be a good-looking man," I finally replied. "I've always thought of him as a good-looking man." And I left her question at that. But truthfully I would be no judge of Stacy's looks at all. He could have tractor-trailer tread marks all over his face and I would hardly notice. I have thirty years of bonding—of shared memories, private jokes, and deep connection—with this man.

Even in the physiology of sex, you can see the fingerprints of God and the intentional way he brings a man and woman together. For example, clinical research shows that for the first eighteen months of marriage, couples have elevated hormones coursing through their bodies, providing a kind of "romance cocktail" that makes it very difficult to get to work on time. Sex is the major event, and it happens with stunning frequency. One of those hormones, oxytocin, promotes feelings of closeness and intimacy between two people.[4] And during sex, oxytocin jumps to five times its normal level.

Every physical aspect of their being conspires to bring them together and to give them great pleasure in the process.

That's how invested God is in bringing a man and a woman together.

A BOND — WHETHER YOU WANT IT OR NOT

What we are looking at here are the laws of the relational universe. Sex creates a bond with another person, whether this was our intention or not. That bond remains, even when the encounter—or the relationship—is long gone.

Women, especially, spend a lot of energy trying to convince themselves that sex should not matter so much. They ought to be able to slough it off. As one woman explained, "I kept watching the way my roommate could just 'do' one man this week and another the next. I tried to become as dispassionate as she was—to treat sex like it was nothing more than frosting on the cake of a great party or a nice dinner out." She was actually relieved to think that maybe she was the normal woman and there was something wrong with cutting your heart and soul off from your body.

When Mary met Steve, he was leading music in the singles group at her church. She was a bit shy, and she admired the way he could be at ease in a crowd. Before long they did almost everything together. Steve said he had never met anyone like Mary. Neither of them intended for the relationship to get sexual, but it did. Once her affection was sealed, he began to flirt with other women and to be irritated by any show of jealousy or suspicion on her part. It all came to a head when one of Mary's friends confessed that Steve had been calling her, suggesting they go out.

Mary kept trying to work things out, but when she finally

realized the relationship was over, she dissolved in a pile of tears and anger. Steve couldn't understand why she felt so disappointed and ashamed. Why couldn't she just move on peaceably? "What's wrong with you?" he asked. "Are you crazy or something?"

The word *crazy* drove Mary's pain underground in a big way. She moved on to other relationships with men, all of which included sex, trying to prove to herself that she was normal—meaning mature and indifferent. She did not like the woman she was becoming.

I was the first person in Mary's life to say the obvious: "Of course you were crushed. Of course you felt enormous pain." It's totally understandable. You can't share this kind of intimacy with a man and brush it off lightly—not without becoming dead on the inside. The bonding aspect of sex is so real that outside its rightful context it becomes a form of bondage, leaving an imprint on the larger personality that takes time to work through. It affects your ability to trust and your readiness to share your real self with someone in a close relationship.

The same principle holds true in the physical world. If you try to pull apart two objects that have been glued together, parts of one will be stuck to the other. Both will show the scars of being torn apart. The world of relationships is no different. Your heart and soul will follow your body. If a connection to a man is made and broken—made and broken again and again—you may lose your capacity to bond to someone deeply. Like glue that has been squeezed out of a tube, everything inside has been spent and you feel numb.

God, in his mercy, longs to restore our souls. And the

truth is that because he authored the mystery of sexuality, only he can restore our souls. Only God can touch the same deep places in you that are awakened in the experience of sex. He made you. The deep places of your soul belong to him first. He gathers up the fragmented pieces of our shattered dreams—of our very selves—and knits them back together, and when he does, it feels like a small miracle.

WHAT SEX IS MEANT TO DO

Sex, in the context God designed it for, touches the core of who we are. It touches our deepest longing: *to be known as we really are and still be loved*. Many people would admit that sex is the most tangible experience they know of feeling loved and wanted by another person. In a true sense, sex in marriage is a lot like the experience of God's grace. You are loved by this person even on the days you don't deserve to be.

I am reminded of all that happens in sexual intimacy when I read a passage out of the life of Isaac, Abraham's son. Isaac's mother, Sarah, had just died, and the whole community was mourning her death. The book of Genesis gives a touching glimpse at what brought Isaac comfort. "Isaac brought [Rebekah] into the tent of his mother Sarah, and he married Rebekah. So she became his wife, and he loved her; and Isaac was comforted after his mother's death."[5]

Comfort, pleasure, a sense of being deeply known and loved and cared for—who would ever guess that all this is communicated through such a simple physical act. But it is.

Can you sense how much God wants to give you in the experience of sexual intimacy? He places such firm boundaries

around it because there is so much to be had here. If you can
sense the great, good heart of God in this, you will understand
why his desire is to reserve this sort of intimacy as the one
place of human sanctuary in your life where nothing but blessing touches you.[6]

There really is no stranger oxymoron than the phrase
casual sex. Or as author Lauren Winner writes in her book
Real Sex:

> Indeed, one can say that in Christianity's vocabulary
> the only real sex is the sex that happens in a mar-
> riage; the faux sex that goes on outside marriage is
> not really sex at all. The physical coming together
> that happens between two people who are not mar-
> ried is only a distorted imitation of sex, as Walt Dis-
> ney's Wilderness Lodge Resort is only a simulation
> of real wilderness. The danger is that when we spend
> too much time in the simulations, we lose the capac-
> ity to distinguish between the ersatz and the real.[7]

BEING IN A BODY

Understanding how a man and a woman are bonded in the
sexual experience is really built on the significance of the
body itself. The mystery hinges on the reality that you and I
were given a body, one cell of which is as complex as New
York City. We are housed in flesh and blood.

We tend to treat the body with much less importance
than God does. To us, it's more like an engine to keep oiled
and running. Or a vehicle that provides us pleasure through

eating and sex. Or a shape we live inside that needs to be sufficiently thin and attractive. And then, when we die, we dissolve into nothingness, or as Beatle George Harrison insisted shortly before his death, "The universe is a great ocean, and I am a drop of water heading back there."[8]

Understanding how a man and a woman are bonded in the sexual experience is really built on the significance of the body itself.

Christianity is unique in its startling claim that you are far more than a drop of water heading back to the ocean. Your very body is telling you something of the mystery that you belong to a God who made himself known in skin and bones—in Jesus Christ. Think of all the ways God could have chosen to make his glory known. In the Old Testament, he placed his glory in a tabernacle and in a pillar of cloud and fire that led Israel in the desert. When God visited his creation, he could have chosen to dwell in a mountain or a dolphin or a holy book. But God came as a man, in a body. "The incarnation forever hallows the flesh," early twentieth-century British lay theologian Charles Williams once said.[9] The living God revealed himself in a body, and what we do with our bodies matters.

This is why missionaries who went to Africa in the 1800s built hospitals and not just churches. Bodies were important. And when Christianity took root in Rome, Christians began to bury their dead and not just burn bodies, as the Romans had always done. Jesus promised to one day raise our bodies in such a way that we will be able to recognize each other after death.

From this perspective, then, it makes sense that the Bible describes sexual promiscuity as a form of suicide. "Flee from sexual immorality," it urges. "All other sins people commit are outside their bodies, but those who sin sexually sin against their own bodies."[10] Promiscuity is like pulling out a gun and shooting off your foot. God lays claim to our bodies as well as our souls. "Do you not know that your bodies are temples of the Holy Spirit? ... You are not your own."[11]

So sex is always more than just sex. You and I cannot engage in something with our bodies without our hearts and souls being affected. A man and a woman's passionate longing to be together in a sexual relationship is their greatest clue to how fervently they long for God; the pleasure they bring each other honors him! In most other major world religions, to be more spiritual is to be less sexual, but not so in Christianity.

Our grandparents understood this mystery better than we do. Part of their wedding vows included these amazing words: "With my body I thee worship." Mike Mason wrote the following in his wonderful book about the mystery of the body in marriage:

> Only when we perceive that nakedness is as close as most of us will ever get to seeing God in the flesh, that these poor bodies of ours are the natural (as opposed to supernatural) expression of God's glory, only then can we begin to understand also that sex is the closest thing to touching Him: that is, next to the Eucharist itself.[12]

THE HEART OF THE MYSTERY

Any really great mystery has a climax that unlocks an important secret and takes you to the heart of the story and leaves you with a touch of awe.

The mystery of what happens in relationships, specifically in sexual intimacy, is no different. Follow me behind the scenes so you can see what is rarely recognized but is really happening.

This drama between a man and a woman plays out against a much larger backdrop. God is telling a story here — his story. He wrote this romance in its original form. Ultimately, it is his heart that searches hill and dale for the one he loves. We find it hard to grasp, but every page of Scripture says the same thing: *We are the ones he is seeking.* Out of the garbage heap of our lives, he claims us as his own — as his bride. Unbelievably, this is his great joy:

> "The LORD your God is in your midst,
> *A victorious warrior.*
> *He will exult over you with joy*
> *He will be quiet in His love,*
> *He will rejoice over you with shouts of joy.*"[13]

The union of a man and woman is only part of the tale being told. The story behind the story is that this is a picture of the union God desires to have with us. This is the real intimacy we were made for and one day will actually know. Author John Eldredge makes this observation: "God turns the universe on its head when he tells us that this is what *he* is seeking with *us*. In fact, Paul says that this is why God created gender and sexuality and marriage — to serve as a living metaphor."[14] All the imagery of the marriage feast of the Lamb leads here: "'For this reason a man will leave his father and mother and be united to his wife, and the two will become one flesh.' This is a profound mystery—but I am talking about Christ and the church."[15]

Have you thought about sex as a metaphor for something larger—as a clue to the oneness God desires with you? Or do you see some sort of fire wall between sexual intimacy and the worship of God? There are uncanny parallels between the two. Sexuality and spirituality serve as bookends on your life as a woman. They both touch the deepest longings of your heart. One gives profound insight into the other. That's why the Song of Songs, the Bible's unvarnished romance story, is part of the *Wisdom* Literature of the Old Testament. There are some things about God we will know only through experiencing the love between a man and a woman. And we will never know ourselves or know another person deeply without being connected to the God who called us into being. It is all part of the same mystery.

> *We are never truly free until our hearts are ravished in the love of God. This is what the mystery of sex has been trying to tell us all along.*

No writer communicated this parallel more clearly than the sixteenth-century poet John Donne. Known in his younger days for vivid love poetry, Donne eventually wrote about God in much the same vein. God, he realized, was the first object of his passion:

> *Yet dearly I love you, and would be lovèd fain,*
> *But am betrothed unto your enemy;*
> *Divorce me, untie, or break that knot again,*
> *Take me to you, imprison me, for I*

Except you enthrall me, never shall be free;
Nor ever chaste, except you ravish me.[16]

If you did not know this poem was about God, would you not assume he was describing love between a man and a woman? But no, Donne is captivated by the larger love story. We are betrothed, lost in an affair with the enemy, he says, hopeless to free ourselves until God enthralls us, until he ravishes our souls with his love.

When you stand back and really think about a relationship with a man and a relationship with God, you realize how one mirrors the other. What is worship, for example, without passion and surrender, the laying bare of the soul before God, with whom you have an exclusive relationship? Real intimacy in sex is based on trust and faithfulness. Aren't those the same qualities at the heart of one's relationship with God?

At the heart of the mystery of sex is a God who pursues you to the end of the earth, not to pin you into submission, but to embrace you at the core of your being with a love beyond that of any man, a love that penetrates to your deepest fears and heals your shame, a love that will not let you go. We are never truly free until our hearts are ravished in the love of God. This is what the mystery of sex has been trying to tell us all along.

Here's the great irony of it all: The love of a man seems real because it's tangible. There are strong arms to hold us. *But.* But the best human love is a mirror, a passageway into the love of God—a love that, while it's not tangible, is far more real. It is the only love that never dies, that never lets go.

FINDING THE SOUL IN SEX

For many women who begin to have sex outside marriage, the first clue they have to the soulish nature of it all is pain. You can't explain messy emotions like jealousy and feeling betrayed without there being a real woman in you who longs for more. This awakening is your soul rolling over and crying to be heard.

In their pursuit of a sexually pure lifestyle, most women find that this connection between soul and body is vital. They must move deeper into the mystery to become free of the bondage of immorality. One woman explains how she began to make the connections inside her:

> I wish someone had told me there is an incredibly fine line between sensuality and spirituality. That I have this deep, deep place inside of me that desperately longs for God, and that because of this fine line I would often try to touch this spot through sensual means—sometimes through binge eating, hoping that if I cram enough food down, I would hit the spot and feel full and satisfied; or at other times, I'd search for a penis to reach this unreachable void.[17]

At the risk of sounding crude, she explains that facing her sensual desires was crucial, because buried in them was her longing for God. And when she moved in the direction of what she really longed for, sexual purity became a free choice she was making for the first time in her life. Out of a growing intimacy with God, she was making a choice, not against sex, but for the strength and dignity that belonged to her as a woman made in God's image. *That is freedom.*

If there were no larger story, no deep mystery between us and God, there would be no such thing as promiscuity. I could sleep with my husband's best friend and feel no more guilt than when I truly enjoy a slice of banana cream pie. It's just a pleasure to be had.

If there were no larger story, you and I could stroll down the backstreets of Amsterdam—a culture even more extreme than ours, where women sit in glass storefronts like any other commodity on the open market, half dressed, waiting to see which men will pay to have sex with them—and we would not be offended. We would not feel nauseous, like we wanted to smash in the glass and take them all home, if there were no larger story.

But there *is* a larger story. You and I are not generic beings, as though God took a cup of soul and poured it into whatever container he could find. We are women created in his very image—made as women, not men. Something in us will always cry out for this reality to be honored. We will forever crave the refuge of relaxing in the arms of a man who has committed his heart and his future to us. Something in us knows that the female body we inhabit is truly the work of an Artist, that the same God who created such beauty cares deeply about the beauty of relationship.

If we listen to the true murmurings of our heart, we will be carried at one and the same time to God and to the rightful embrace of our restored sexuality.

Questions for Discussion and Reflection

1. How has this chapter changed your view of the role that sexual intimacy is meant to play in a woman's life?

2. God's intention is to bond a man and a woman for a lifetime through the experience of sexual intimacy. What part of this mystery is a new thought to you? What are some of the implications for your life?

3. What would it be like to have a sexual relationship with a man that was so free, so absent of guilt and shame that you could openly acknowledge God there with you?

4. What impact does it have on you to realize that God pursues you to the end of the earth, not to pin you into submission, but to lavish his love on you?

5. Is the idea that your longing for God is buried in your sensual desires new to you? What are the implications for your life?

8

Getting Back Your Heart

I slept with three other men before I was married, but now that I am, I wish that my husband was the only one. Once you find someone you really love—someone you want to spend your life with—the others don't mean a thing. The memories almost make you ill.

— CLARA, AGE ΥΛ

"But for you who revere my name, the sun of righteousness will rise with healing in its wings. And you will go out and leap like calves released from the stall."

— MALACHI ٤:٢

*S*exual intimacy could be likened to a treasure chest. Inside is a wealth of desirable things, even beyond the sheer physical pleasure of the experience. There's a sense of refuge in feeling known by someone, moments of oneness that so rival anything on this planet that it's not hard to imagine them as a tiny sample of the union you most desire—union with God himself. Sex is a touch of healing on the very old ache of incompleteness we carry in our broken, solitary selves.

Then why all the fuss?

If so much is possible in a love relationship turned sexual, or in a sexual relationship, period, then is God being the ultimate Scrooge to place this experience within the bonds of marriage and to prescribe it as a gift for one man and one woman as they move through life together? Isn't this rather like withholding a trip to Disneyland from a bunch of orphans?

It looks that way at first glance. Certainly a lot of people see sex and all it provides as a natural progression of events, a romantic tryst to which we are entitled as human beings. Everywhere you look there are books and magazines offering tips on how to provide the ultimate sexual experience to make your life complete.

Oh, that they would tell the rest of the story—the morning-after story! The tale of sheepishly walking back to your dorm or apartment, trying to slip in unnoticed. The regret of discovering there is no future with the man, no love to share forever. There is a dark side to the mystery of sexuality, and thousands of women can give witness to feelings we never expected to feel.

As much potential as sexual intimacy has in a marriage to bless and bond a couple, it has, outside the union of a husband and a wife, a commensurate ability to create havoc. It brings not life and love but bondage. The phrase often used is *soul tie*, meaning that married or not, starry-eyed lovers or casual acquaintances, two individuals are knit together in ways that affect them long after their sexual encounter. Something transpires between them, on a spiritual level at least, that bleeds over into other relationships and other parts of their lives.

When an unhealthy soul tie forms, the relationship breeds not union and fellowship as God intended but rather control and fear. Those two emotions grow like a virus in the petri dish of immorality. Lisa Bevere points out:

> This same principle [of unhealthy soul ties] makes it very difficult for sexually broken or violated women to stand strong in the face of temptation. They have a hard time saying no even when they want to. They are overwhelmed with either lust or guilt, and often both.... They become victims and a magnet for sexual abuse and promiscuity.[1]

Soul ties with men in your past can resurface in totally unexpected ways. Listen as one woman describes in her journal a period in her late twenties when the sexual connections of her past began to rattle around like ghosts in the cupboard:

> Why on earth am I starting to have these 3-D memories of men I've been with sexually — some of them years ago now? OK, so I'm lonely these days. I'm stressed. What else is new? But like a recurring viral sore on my lip, these memories take hold of my imagination and I'm gone. Always, it leaves me with

a vague feeling of guilt, a hollow dissatisfaction with my life, and a greater sexual hunger. They change my perception of myself toward an inward self-consciousness that slows me down, pulls me away from God and other people—and deeper into myself. I want out. I am plagued with the feeling that I gave away more of myself than I can get back—and in at least a couple of instances, I got more of a guy than I ever really wanted.

This woman is describing a common trinity of emotions that often washes up on the shores of past sexual encounters. There are feelings of guilt, a hollow dissatisfaction that is hard to pin down, and greater sexual hunger—a need for something to fill the void.

Let me offer an example of this kind of bondage from my own life. For years after I married, I had the same dream over and over. Always it was my wedding day, and I was standing at the end of a long church aisle. Some kind of fog or haze filled the sanctuary. I could not, for the life of me, see the face of the man I was marrying. Who was waiting for me at the front of this church—Stacy or a guy I had dated for four years previously? I stood there helplessly trying to see through the fog. *Who was I marrying?* The confusion and panic built, and finally I woke up. Always the same sense of relief overwhelmed me as I realized that the man next to me was indeed Stacy. I had married the "right" guy.

I believe that my dream (which has been the only recurrent one in my life) was the result of the soul connection I had forged over four years in a previous relationship. While

Stacy and I were both virgins when we married, I knew I had been too physically involved with this earlier guy. I knew it at the time. The bondage of the guilt I felt—and my inability to break the pattern—was in large part what brought me to Christ. I could not break free on my own.

This is the way a soul tie works. We think of an old relationship (or relationships) as history. Perhaps we haven't even thought about it in years, but the residue remains. It surfaces in our insecurity, the vigilant bracing of ourselves in fear of being hurt again. It pronounces judgment over our lovableness, as though we don't deserve the affection of a good man. It mutates into a drive to please: *Just tell me what kind of woman you want, and I will become her.*

Or sometimes, as in my case, it reappears in something as strange as a dream that won't go away. Lingering soul ties from a woman's past have their own ways of becoming visible.

BREAKING FREE OF BONDAGE

Growing up, Suzanne was known as the good girl. She was the only first grader who never got "a worm of misbehavior" pinned on her apple, the teenager who drove her friends home safely when they had too much to drink, the college student who studied way before the test.

When she landed a job in the big city after graduation, her friends warned her: "This is going to be a whole new ball game." She was leaving the warm shelter of a small church-affiliated college in New Hampshire to join a nationally ranked architectural firm in Chicago. But, hey, she told them, she'd keep her eyes open. This was just too good a career move to pass up.

It truly was an amazing opportunity. With so much business coming through the front door, Suzanne got the chance to learn on the job, with more and more responsibility invested in her. The managing partners called her "the whiz kid." So she didn't think twice when one of them invited her to attend a marketing conference with him in New York.

She has replayed the scene in her mind so many times now, always looking for the place where she should have seen what was coming. Maybe it was the second glass of wine at dinner that clouded her judgment. Surely things were getting dicey when he walked her back to her room, but she was totally floored when he suddenly crossed the threshold and then closed and locked the door behind him. What she regrets most was that she couldn't summon the words *Get out*. It just seemed so out of line to say those words to a man you would technically call your boss, and Suzanne had never been one to make a scene.

She couldn't exactly call what happened between them rape. It was a power play to be sure, but one she agreed to as though walking through a dream. She felt as though she had been stung by a stun gun. This man had a wife and three children at home. And here he was, coming on to her.

This was their little secret, he said afterward. It never happened again, because Suzanne was too smart to let it. She had purchased her education in the fires of regret. The incident was never mentioned between them. They went on from there—boss and employee, seasoned professional and new kid on the block—with her eyes wide open. But for

Suzanne it was a major turning point. What difference did it make now whom she got involved with? At least that was the way she felt. From then on, having a relationship with a man invariably turned into a relationship that included sex.

One's sexual past can come in many different shapes and flavors. Suzanne's has a flare of the dramatic, a story fit for a novel. Your experience may be a world away from hers. Perhaps you became sexually involved with a guy you really loved and with whom you shared affection and hope for a future together. That is often the case. Somehow things just didn't work out. Or maybe sexual purity was something you came to value only after you lost it—or perhaps after you realized that it was part of having a relationship with God.

When a woman sees a future with a man to whom she longs to be able to give her heart, she may suddenly become aware that her heart is technically no longer hers. It has been shattered in pieces, enjoyed by other men whose faces are preserved only in scrapbooks. As Clara said, once you find someone with whom you want to spend your life, you wish there were no memories of previous men.

So what do you do with a sexual past in order to have a genuine fresh start?

GOING BACK BEFORE YOU GO ON

The concept of what has come to be called *renewed virginity* has attracted great interest.[2] At least in terms of our innermost being, we can recover an innocence of soul, a regathering of our heart, an inner cleansing that brings wholeness. This kind of inner restoration is inherently a spiritual process.

Sometimes when I am talking with a woman who wants a clean start in life, I wish that I had a giant eraser in my hand capable of wiping the slate clean in an instant. But the only process that works is really much better than a magic wand or a giant eraser. It brings women to the only one who can heal and make whole. It isn't that complicated. It is simply a means by which you can come to terms with your sexual history. Almost any sexual act with a man, especially one that involves a degree of nakedness (such as oral sex or heavy sexual intimacy), will feel like a bond that needs to be broken.

> *Whatever your sexual history is, the power to break free from the past is not in you or even in the process. The power of God is the only force that can set you free.*

It is important to realize that whatever your sexual history is, the power to break free from the past is not in you or even in the process. The power of God is the only force that can set you free. I'm talking about the same quiet yet earth-shattering power that raised Jesus from the dead being brought to bear on this one dark corner of your life—a corner God cares deeply about. The apostle Paul had experienced God's power and prayed that believers would know it: "I pray that the eyes of your heart may be enlightened in order that you may know the hope to which he has called you, the riches of his glorious inheritance in his people, *and his incomparably great power for us who believe.*"[3]

In preparation, you may want to spend some time fasting. You will find that fasting is amazingly helpful for focusing the heart on God and breaking spiritual bondages.[4] You may choose to fast from solid food for a day or from a series of meals over a longer period of time—whatever seems appropriate. Through Isaiah the Lord reminded his people of the power of fasting.

> *"Is not this the kind of fasting I have chosen:*
> *to loose the chains of injustice*
> *   and untie the cords of the yoke,*
> *to set the oppressed free*
> *   and break every yoke?"*[5]

On the day you choose to deal with your past, set aside at least a couple of hours during which you will not be interrupted. With paper, pen or pencil, and Bible in hand, find a place where you can be alone. When you are finished, you may want to ask a spiritual friend with whom you feel safe to pray with you.

As you begin the healing process, spend some time in praise and worship. Music helps immensely, and reading praise psalms out loud is a classic way to enter God's presence (Psalms 90 to 100 are especially good). Praise and thank God until you can sense that he is right there in the middle of the muck and mire with you. He is, indeed.

Remember that you are not alone in this experience. Jesus is our Advocate before the Father. He is our High Priest "who has been tempted in every way, just as we are—yet was without sin."[6] This means that Jesus, in ways we can't comprehend, knows and understands sexual temptation. He pleads your case before God. He takes the weight of your sin on his own shoulders. He bears the curse of your sin so that you don't have to feel its sting all your days—that you can instead experience the blessing of God.[7]

Your image of God as you enter this time is important. He is not aloof and removed, doling out small pieces of his favor if you say the right words. He, too, has been waiting for this moment—waiting for you to wait on him, to look for a deliverance that only he can give.

> The LORD longs to be gracious to you;
>   he rises to show you compassion.
> For the LORD is a God of justice.
>   Blessed are all who wait for him![8]

The next part of this process may take a bit of time. The Bible says that the truth will set us free,[9] but sometimes the truth has to be pretty specific. This is where a pencil and a blank pad of paper come into the picture. The truth you know but don't consciously recognize has a wonderful way of slipping out on paper. As you begin to write, ask God to show you what you experienced and, most important, what you came to believe about yourself, about men, and about God in this place where your soul was opened prematurely to another person through a sexual encounter.

Sex is meant to bring about healing in our lives, but expressed in promiscuity, sex (or even pseudo-sex) brings a wounding of some sort—pain that follows on its heels and leaves a hole in our lives. In this wound, a lie inevitably takes up residence. We believe this lie, whether it is about ourselves, about God, or about men. And when this lie sits in our soul and festers, it becomes a lens that alters our perspective. We start to "see" life through the lens of these lies. This is the unholy sequence: *a wound that gives birth to a lie that turns into a lens through which we see life and relationships in a distorted way.*

WRITE ABOUT EACH OF THE MEN IN YOUR LIFE

- What drew you into this sexual relationship?

   I think Matt came along at a time in my life when I particularly needed male attention. With my father having left a few years before, it just felt so amazingly good to have a guy single me out. I felt wanted and appreciated for the first time in a long while.

- What was the negative emotional and spiritual impact?

   I tried to go on as though nothing much had happened. But I hated myself for what I'd done with him. I turned kind of hard after Matt, determined that I'd get out before the next man decided to. And I felt like I was just going through the motions with God— like he was on another planet.

- How did the relationship affect the way you saw yourself and God and other men? (What are the lies you believed?)

   After Matt, I saw myself as a woman who didn't quite have what it took to keep a man interested in her. I was the one left behind, the one who just wanted too much from a guy. I was, supposedly, impossible to

*please. And it felt like God wasn't all that interested
in me either! I guess I saw him as not caring what
happened from this point. It was all up to me to find
the love I longed for.*

Some women find they write pages and pages. Others,
like this one, say what they need to say in a few sentences. The
part that surprised this woman was the
judgment she passed on herself after
she and Matt broke up: she must be
a woman who is impossible to please,
who wants too much from a man. This
is actually the opposite of the truth.
It's the lie she swallowed in her pain.
After Matt, her real problem was accepting poor treatment
from guys, taking almost anything someone threw her way.

> A wound gives birth
> to a lie that turns into a
> lens through which we
> see life and relationships
> in a distorted way.

Our pain often gets projected onto God, as though he
caused it or doesn't care. The worst part of promiscuity is
the sense of spiritual and emotional isolation it causes. At the
very point where we most need the comfort of a good Father,
we don't feel we can go to him.

It may also help you to write a letter (which you don't
send) to any man with whom you feel a deep connection.
Write about the anger, the regret, the grief you feel. Write
until there's nothing more left to write. Then put the letter
down for a week. When you return, write another (perhaps
shorter) letter (again, which you don't send) in which you
extend forgiveness. Forgiveness is the major way in which we
let go of the lies we've believed about ourselves, about men,
about God.[10]

PRAY ABOUT EACH OF THE MEN IN YOUR LIFE

Nothing feels cleaner than a prayer of repentance. Essentially you are laying down the pain, the lies you believed, and the choice you made to get sexually involved with each man you have written about. I wish I could convey how much it helps to pray through what you have written with a friend, therapist, pastor, or spiritual director. Receiving Communion is also an active way of applying the sacrifice of Jesus Christ, his body and blood, to this corner of your life where it is most needed.

What is important is that there is a living, breathing witness to your change of heart, to the breaking of a connection that never should have been. If at all possible, bring someone into the fight with you. The apostle James offers this simple, timeless remedy: "Confess your sins to each other and pray for each other so that you may be healed."[11]

In praying through each of these relationships, you are offering yourself afresh to God so that he can restore the broken places in your soul by his mercy and power. You are asking him on the merits of Jesus Christ to break any remaining ties or bondage in your life from these relationships. You are asking for his forgiveness. And because there is nothing more binding to your soul than unforgiveness, you are offering forgiveness to any man you may need to forgive.

In the name of Jesus and by the power that raised him from the dead, I ask you, Lord, to sever whatever negative spiritual and emotional ties were created in the promiscuity of this relationship.

and renounce my sin and the idolatry of
my love over yours.

I ask you to speak truth to the deepest part of me,
and I renounce the lie [name the lie] I believed as a
result of this experience. Knowing your willingness to
forgive me, I offer this same forgiveness to the man/men
with whom I have been involved.

I ask your Spirit to cleanse me from every promis-
cuous image, every ungodly thought. Please gather up
every fragment of my soul and make me whole again.
Make me, above all, yours.

I praise you for your mercy, and I claim, in Jesus
Christ, the freedom and power to lay hold of my des-
tiny as a daughter of the living God.

Amen.

God will lead you as you pray. This is a holy moment in
your life, more significant than you can now imagine. When
you have finished praying about a particular relationship,
tear up the page you have written—or burn it—as a sym-
bolic way of letting go of the past.

What a woman often finds in this process is that once
she has prayed through the promiscuous aspect of a previous
relationship, she is able to retrieve the best parts and take
them forward with her. In other words, that Jim made her
feel like a million bucks because he loved her sense of humor,
or Dillon taught her to ski, or Tony opened the world of poli-
tics to her—all these are good gifts she can now keep freely.
In a very practical sense, God's heart is always *to redeem*—to
reach into the fire of our own making and by his mercy pull

out the good. Only God can bring blessing where we have sown curses.

When you are finished praying through the relationships you have written about, you may want to read Psalm 116, a psalm that amazingly gathers up the pieces of this time. Psalm 116 was obviously written by a kindred spirit; you will recognize his words as the cry of your own heart. Read the psalm through a couple of times. If you want it to come alive in a special way, try writing it in your own words:

> *I do love you, Lord, because you hear my prayer.*
> *You turn your ear toward me,*
>   *so I will call on you as long as I live.*
> *Death was all around me;*
>   *my life was a mess.*
> *I had nowhere to turn until I called on you.*
>   *You are the one who has saved my life.*
>
>   Psalm 116:1–4, my paraphrase

THE DOOR OF HOPE

Only slowly over time did it dawn on me what the sensuality of my past had cost me. I thought it was something I left behind like a sweater two sizes too small. Years after I married, though, I would have flashes of insight into the awesome overlap between body and soul. I would see this "other altar" I had worshiped at when I was willing to dole out myself in small pieces for the sake of a man's affection. I would see that I had offered my heart to another god.

When you peel back the edges of promiscuity, what stares

back at you is the shape of an idol. We are asking a man to serve as a stand-in god who will fill us or rescue us and give our life meaning, if only for a while, through the illusion of love a sexual connection brings. We are preferring another god, in the form of a flesh and blood person, to the intimacy of God. In C. S. Lewis's terms, we are living in a "bent" state. Leaning in toward another, we try very hard to draw our sense of *life* from him.

This is not the way God made us. You and I are created to stand up straight. We are meant to live with our eyes turned toward Jesus to receive all good things from him—even a man. The wonder of the gospel is that it removes the barrier between us and God. He is actually the one who lifts our heads and invites us into life. Two words shed special light on this process of the reclaiming of your heart: *repentance* and *renouncing*.

Repentance means that I agree with God about a particular sin or habit or attitude in my life. I am no longer trying to hide or pretend. I am willing to give my sin over to God rather than repress it and stuff it down inside. Repentance straightens me up. I am *coram deo*, living before the face of God.

Renouncing is an even stronger word and thus is especially freeing. When you pray, "I renounce this habit or attitude or behavior," you are serving notice. It's like saying, "I close the door of my soul to this sin. It is no longer welcome, and whenever it rears its head again, my stated policy is that I will not invite it to have a place in my life."

I used to shy away from such words as *repentance* and *renouncing* until I grasped more of the love and mercy of God in my own life. The crucial thing is being in a place where your face is lifted up again and the shower of God's love is pouring down on your broken soul. His goodness is so lavish, the big questions are: Am I able to receive from him? Can I allow myself to live in the freedom of knowing myself as a woman accepted and loved by God? Repentance is meant to open locked gates in our souls.

Our sexual past is not something most of us think of bringing to God in prayer. We hope to keep that sort of thing locked away, especially from God. It doesn't seem that we could survive his gaze on this part of our lives. And this, then, is what makes you feel as though you are in pieces, your sexuality divorced from your spirituality in ways that leave you feeling half alive. God's mercy would make you a whole woman and able to offer your heart to a man you love.

When God's love embraces your shame and regret, it always comes as a surprise. For he meets you, not with the wrath you expect, but with his undeserved kindness. Through the pain you encounter by your own willful choices, he draws you to a place where you can finally—finally—hear his voice. His voice is firm but gentle. He does not point his finger in condemnation. Rather, right in the middle of the mess you have made, he carves a door of hope and pours his very life in and through you. He gives you beauty instead of the ashes of shame and failure. He makes new.

Through the pain you encounter by your own willful choices, he draws you to a place where you can finally hear his voice.

From the narrow restraints of our sexual choices, we skip like "calves released from the stall."[12] The whole pasture of our sexuality, as a woman loved by God, is ours again to enjoy and to give.

In a thousand varied ways, Scripture says all this, and never more clearly than the voice of God through the prophet Hosea:

> "Therefore I am now going to allure her,
>   I will lead her into the desert
>   and speak tenderly to her.
> There I will give her back her vineyards,
>   and will make the Valley of Achor* a door of hope.
> There she will sing as in the days of her youth,
>   as in the day she came up out of Egypt."[13]

WHAT GOD DOES

Let me close with the story of two sisters who competed for the love of the same man. Their story is the stage God uses to tell an even greater tale — a tale that pictures the way God is at work in you.

Here's how the story of these two sisters plays out.[14] Rachel was the beautiful one. Leah had "weak eyes," as the story goes, meaning she wasn't known for the way she looked. Her younger sister was the one who stopped traffic.

Jacob fell madly in love with the beautiful sister, Rachel, while he worked for her father. And in the manner of the day, he agreed to work for her father seven years in order to

---

* The Valley of Achor is "the valley of trouble" and invokes the memory of some of Israel's most flagrant sins (see Joshua 7:26).

marry her. Jacob put in his time, so to speak, and these seven years "seemed like only a few days to him because of his love for her."[15]

So the wedding was finally on; the day came for Rachel to become Jacob's bride. But Leah was the oldest daughter, the one who should be married first. You have to wonder what Jacob drank at the reception, because his father-in-law was able to pull off the switch of all switches. Jacob went to bed that night with his bride, only to discover in the morning that the woman lying next to him was not Rachel; it was Leah. Jacob had married Leah.

Can you imagine the humiliation of being Leah and having some man roll over and groan when he realizes it's you? You are not the woman he intended to wake up beside.

Jacob is undaunted. He keeps Leah as a wife, but he works another seven years so he can marry the woman of his dreams, Rachel. Leah is not to be outdone, though. She conceives a child before Rachel does and in one of the more poignant lines of Scripture, she says, "Surely my husband will love me now."[16] She bore Jacob not one son — but six. And each time she thought he would finally, finally love her.

But those sons didn't change a thing. Jacob loved Rachel, the beautiful woman he had set his heart on from the beginning. Leah never had a chance, really. She could barter her son's mandrakes; she could compete until the cows came home. Jacob loved Rachel. That's how this story begins — that's how it ends.

The important part, though, is where God comes in later on in this story. When God was looking down the trail of human history to choose a line of people through whom he would send his son, he didn't choose Rachel's heirs. God is not found among "the beautiful people." No, God sent his son through Leah's lineage. This woman who was no one's first choice—the girl not asked to the prom—was the one God chose to be the great-great-great grandmother in the royal lineage of his Son.

The message is one I hope you will pull into some place deep inside you. None of us feel like "the beautiful woman," do we? We are a lot more Leah than Rachel. A past of sexual regret only increases our sense of ugliness.

But when God comes into the center of our shame, he accomplishes the great exchange. He takes all of our ugliness on himself, and he gives us his beauty in return. It's too amazing, really. But that is what happens. He takes our shame and clothes us in his beauty. This is the larger point from the story of Leah and Rachel[17]. And it's the story God would write in each of us.

> God made Him who knew no sin to become sin on our behalf, so that we might become the righteousness of God in Him.
>
> 2 Corinthians 5:2 NASB

Questions for Discussion and Reflection

1. As you read this chapter, what kind of thoughts and emotions did it evoke in you? They could be any one of a number of emotions:

   • fear
   • anger
   • discouragement
   • sorrow
   • regret
   • hope
   • longing

2. How would you describe what a soul tie, made through some kind of strong emotional or sexual involvement with a man, has felt like in your life?

3. What kind of fallout or residue or effect have you experienced from this soul tie?

4. When do you experience the longing to have a truly fresh start?

5. Finish this thought: When I think about embracing the love of God in this part of my life, I feel _____ _____.

9

Recognizing a Good Man

Victim of love, it's such an easy part
And you know how to play it so well....
You're walking the wire, pain and desire,
Looking for love in between.

—THE EAGLES, "VICTIM OF LOVE"

A s soon as Alexa walked through the door, I knew something big had happened. She looked noticeably different. Her eyes had an unusual intensity to them. The cause, I suddenly realized, was on her ring finger. Alexa was engaged. I had not seen her for a year, and I was eager to hear her story.

"Tell me about this guy," I said, congratulating her. "How did this come about?"

The story came tumbling out. Alexa had worked alongside

Ben for months in a coffee shop where she worked part-time while she went to graduate school. He was between banking jobs. Slowly their friendship had ripened into something more—something she felt she could build a life around.

Then I asked the question that Alexa surely knew I would ask. Knowing the men in her past and her profound sense of regret and disappointment, what made Ben different? What made her feel that this man was the love of a lifetime?

"Oh—Ben," she said, shaking her head. "You wouldn't believe how well he treats me." Her answer cheered my soul. She began to rattle through a list of descriptors. His strength of character. The spine to stand up for his convictions. Loyalty. Compassion. An ability to draw out of her courage she didn't know she had. A hunger for God. Collectively, her descriptors pointed to a guy worthy of her respect. She wanted to marry him.

Being free of a physical relationship, she and Ben had gotten to know each other in many other ways, and their relationship had aged slowly over the course of a year like a bottle of fine wine. Alexa's eyes were wide open, and the more she saw of this man, the more she liked what she saw.

RECOGNIZING A GOOD MAN

Every woman has a dial on the inside that's related to men. That dial is set on "normal." What we get used to relating to in men is what we call "normal." So if we put up with flaky behavior, this becomes the level at which our expectations get set. And normal, of course, just seems normal.

Part of the problem of promiscuity is that it starts to

seem normal, and with that usually comes a host of selfish stuff. We aren't meeting guys we would want to take home to anyone.

What is wonderful in Alexa's story is the way this dial gets reset. It's like she woke up and could actually *see* what a particular guy was made of. She stopped feeling she had to accept whatever came her way. Literally, her sense of "normal" changed. Feeling loved became something much more substantial than being desired sexually.

The good work of God in a woman's life resets this inner dial, piece by piece, until her dignity as a woman is restored. No longer is she willing to take the crumbs, to scrape the bottom of the love barrel. The bar rises on her expectations for a man. Hope works its magic—it helps her discard the mediocre because she senses that God has something better for her. Like a magnet, "good" men are drawn to her positive expectation, and lesser men go where they can get what they want quicker, with less required.

My point is that we each carry around a dial, a compass, that points us in the direction of certain kinds of men. Having this compass set in the right direction determines the men we are drawn to—and the men we attract. Many factors come into play in the setting of this compass—our history with the first man in our life (our father), our first experiences with guys, the places in relationships where we have felt hurt. Our inner compass substantially affects our perspective on men.

Visit for a moment some of the memories and images that may affect the way you see men. For instance, can you remember sitting on your father's lap? Did you, like so many girls, get your dad to teach you how to shoot a hoop or throw a baseball? Who was the first boyfriend who brought you flowers? Was there ever a man you loved who held you when you cried—and just holding you was purely enough?

"True north" in the world of relationships is always about the best God has put in a man brought together with the best God has put in you.

In very good ways, those kinds of memories shape an expectation inside you that serves like a compass to keep you pointed in the direction of men you can trust—men who will offer their strength to shelter you and to do you good. "True north" in the world of relationships is always about the best God has put in a man brought together with the best God has put in you—for a purpose larger than you both.

As God restores the integrity of your heart, you will find that your orientation to men changes in significant ways. God teaches you what to look for in a man. Isaiah wrote about the way God personally leads his children:

> *"I am the LORD your God,*
> *who teaches you what is best for you,*
> *who directs you in the way you should go."*[1]

In other words, God retrains our thinking about what is truly valuable in a relationship and promises to lead us in the way we need to go.

HOW THE COMPASS IS SET

When you think about what you have come to anticipate in men, there is no more important man in the picture than your father. Even if you never knew him, or if he left your life through death or desertion, your father is the first man in your life.

We look into our fathers' eyes as a mirror that tells us we are lovely and valuable as a daughter and as an emerging woman. This begins very early. I remember, for instance, noticing when our daughter turned three how differently she related to Stacy—the innocent thrill of being Daddy's girl, her squeals of delight as she was hoisted above the world on his shoulders. For most of us, our father is the man we first get to "try out" our femininity on.

What you did or did not experience with your father shaped your hope for what you could expect to experience with any man thereafter. He laid down the grid you carried into the larger world.

Many women these days who by the time they become teenagers lost their fathers through death or divorce now realize how that loss propelled them into the arms of whatever guys crossed their paths. Indeed, the tender years of turning from a girl into a young woman are a deeply formative time for the protection and valuing of our sexuality. Many of us later see that accepting the sexual advances of a boyfriend was a poor substitute for wanting a really good talk with Dad.

I don't mean to imply that we can blame our fathers for the poor choices we have made regarding men. We have to own our choices in order to make new ones (for example, "I'm the one who decided to spend the night at John's apartment when I was eighteen"). While a father's absence may shape the hole in our souls, we choose how we will fill it.

Every father, no matter how good or how poor, falls short in some way. Some fail dramatically. We have places of aching need in our souls that even the best father cannot humanly touch. The question that shapes our lives is *where* we take this need. Many of us envision redemption in the shape of a man—a living, breathing person very different from ourselves who seems destined to fill the void.

When I was in my early twenties, I found a startling promise in this regard in the book of Psalms: "My father and my mother have forsaken me, but the LORD will take me up."[2] In other words, if my parents abandon me literally, or if they simply fail me as human beings, God promises to "take me up" in my orphaned state. He will become both father and mother, in the deepest sense of the words. He will do what no man in my life can do.

Growing up, then, whether you are twenty or fifty, is mostly about switching fathers. Your real Father spoke the world into being, yet he also has your name engraved on the palms of his hand. He knows when you lie down and when you arise. He records your tears in his book. Like the best of all possible fathers, he pours the healing oil of his love, if you let him, into the hole in your soul.

HOW DO YOU SEE MEN?

We have seen that each of us carries an internal compass that governs the kind of men we attach to, what we are conditioned to expect, and how we interpret feeling loved. Loving a man sexually and then leaving him or being left by him has a profound effect on our psyche. The repeated making and breaking of sexual bonds tilts our inner compass noticeably off the mark. Let's explore three common distortions that are birthed in relational pain.

An Impossible Dream

Sometimes when a woman's past is littered with broken relationships, she becomes drawn like a magnet to "the impossible man"—the guy who's really not capable of offering anyone much of a relationship. One good conversation, maybe two, and a woman's most appropriate response would be, "Next?" It's time to move on.

Sometimes a woman's past predisposes her toward men who are fundamentally inaccessible. Sarah grew up with a father she greatly admired but who was emotionally out of reach. She could never just sit and carry on a conversation with him. The men Sarah became attracted to were charming and flirtatious; for a while, being with them made Sarah feel like the belle of the ball. But when you scraped off the veneer, the man himself was utterly self-absorbed. He was on again, off again—there only when he felt like it. Sarah, however, was so busy doing his part and hers. She was so convinced her love could heal him that she barely noticed his poor behavior until she was way into the relationship.

Each of us carries an internal compass that governs the kind of men we attach to, what we are conditioned to expect, and how we interpret feeling loved.

As Sarah began to recover her own soul—as God set things right on the inside—she began to explore the nature of *friendship*. What did a give-and-take reciprocity look like in any relationship?

What did it mean to stand back and watch a man until she could see his heart and he had time to prove his worth or lack thereof? Finding true north, for Sarah, involved exploring these questions.

The other thing that radically changed for Sarah was her definition of *exciting*. What she previously called exciting was the breathless way she felt when she had been jerked around. A quote from Robin Norwood's vintage *Women Who Love Too Much* explains this transition:

> She had to learn to simply be in the company of men whose company she considered nice, even if she also found them a little boring ... no bells peal, no rockets explode, no stars fall from heaven.... Because she was used to excitement and pain, struggle and victory or defeat, an interchange that lacked these powerful components felt too tame to be important and unsettling as well.[371]

A Source of Life

The ending of a relationship (even if you are the one who let go) can make the lost object compulsively desirable. Many women go from one man to the next out of a huge fear of being alone. Alone is just not doable. It means you are unwanted, unloved—you are standing out in the cold with your nose pressed against the warm pane of unattainable intimacy. Only a man can make the solitariness go away.

Seeing the other gender as the source of life is a temptation that goes all the way back to the garden of Eden. You can sense it in the bony, blaming fingers that Adam and Eve pointed at each other. The thinking is this: Somehow, if a man (or a woman) were just here for me in the way I need, my life would be OK. All the while, someone is present who knows and understands our solitariness so well that his most common response is, "Do not fear, for I am with you." God has promised to take the toxic awfulness, the shame, out of being "alone."

Suppose the frame around being without a relationship were different. Suppose this was a providential season to get your own stuff together and to discover life—to enjoy the people around you, to get to know God better. Aloneness can be a nontoxic, open space in your life filled with a world of possibility. So many women realize, after they wrestle their fear of aloneness to the floor, that a string of months—or a couple of years—with no man in their life was the best thing that ever happened to them. It gave them "just me" time for their own personal growth.

Coming into a relationship with a man from the emotional vantage point of knowing deep in your soul that you are already loved is liberating. Before any man appeared in your life, you were loved by God. You were given worth and honor by the only one truly worthy of such. To embrace this is to be set free. When you can look at a man and know that he can't give you what you most long for—worth, love, and a sense of identity—then you are free to be loved by him. The most he can ever do (which, in itself, is no small thing) is to give witness to the worth God already invests in you. *But you must claim it first for yourself.*

I am often drawn to the words of a man who spent his life as a single man—the apostle John. In the simplest of phrases, he described himself as "the disciple whom Jesus loved."[4] The love of Jesus was that real to him. Can you imagine being able to describe yourself simply as a woman whom Jesus loves? It is his love that makes the situation of being alone, without a relationship, one that holds its own share of possibilities and life.

Merely a Useful Appendage

The third common distortion is almost the opposite of feeling that life doesn't begin until there is a man in one's life. It is the mentality that men are expendable—and needing one makes you weak.

Women have worked hard not to need men in some of the obvious ways they used to need them. More and more, they have their own paychecks. They own homes, fix the plumbing, mow the grass, and maintain their own cars. They get used to playing hardball with the guys every day in a work setting. It's great to be able to do the things men do well—unless it starts to seem as though your world is stuck there and your softer, more vulnerable side gets lost.

If you add a broken heart into this mix, you can end up really close to seeing men as merely a useful appendage. Some women may say, "Men. Who needs them? They are just one of life's add-ons—useful, especially if you want children down the road. But I'll just concentrate on succeeding in my career and cultivating my own version of the Ya-Ya sisterhood." The strong, independent single woman has become a cultural icon.

Oddly enough, in Christian circles, "not needing anyone" is sometimes mistaken for a virtue, as though godliness were about looking to God alone without any real human touch. But this defies God's plan for you as a woman created for connectedness, with a heart full of longing. It blinds you to the special symmetry that is possible in the presence of a man—no matter the setting. What he brings to the table and what you bring are indeed a sum greater than either part.

Seeing men as something you can do without is usually a response to pain of some sort. Your heart got shut down somewhere along the way. Opening yourself to wanting a man's touch on your life again can feel a bit scary, because doing so carries the possibility of being hurt. Somehow, though, the restorative work of God in a woman's life inevitably leads to this vulnerability that is a part of experiencing real love.

ENJOYING THE PRESENCE OF A REAL MAN

Jasmine met the guy she first slept with in a church youth group in high school. They had not meant to have sex, but once they did, there seemed to be no way back. Besides, they both thought they might eventually want to marry.

What ensued was three years of on-again, off-again attachment during which neither could go forward toward marriage—or backward toward friends. Jasmine grew more and more convinced that she wanted to move on, but something about the physical connection kept her in a place of emotional dependency she could not break. Normally a strong person, she could not picture herself alone without this particular guy.

Jasmine says that when she finally broke off this relationship ("Please don't call me anymore"), she entered a period she could only call *grieving*, similar to what one feels when he or she loses a spouse to death or divorce. She sought refuge in every other friendship she still had, and she gave herself to growing spiritually. Still it took time to heal.

I have heard so many stories like Jasmine's. And it does make sense that a deep connection with a man, one that has been formed sexually, will take time to get beyond. It's like putting your heart in the hospital and giving God the time required to mend it.

If you find that you need time to heal from a relationship, or if you realize that your choice in men comes more out of desperation and pain than it does wisdom, try spending a season of time with no man in your life. Immerse yourself in a relationship with a very different man, one who will never let you down—the Son of Man, Jesus. He is more real than anyone you or I will ever share a meal or a bed with.

I can promise that you will be safe in his company, as have women throughout the ages. You will be valued, protected, and enjoyed. During his years on earth, the women

Throughout the ages women who feel like castoffs, who fear they've screwed up their lives, have found the shelter of a huge rock in Jesus Christ.

who followed him were a collection of everything imaginable. One of his favorites, the first woman to witness his resurrection, had been plagued by demons before she knew his healing touch. Another was the talk of the town, and for good reason. She had known, in the biblical sense, at least six men in her life. Jesus gave her what no man could—a new start, a new identity. Even women like Joanna, whose husband managed the king's business affairs, left her important social life behind so she could follow Jesus from place to place, contributing to his support.

The best explanation for the devotion of these women is that no one ever loved them like he did. Innumerable women would echo just that: "No one ever loved me like Jesus."

There is something amazingly attractive about Jesus as a man. There has to be, because throughout the ages women who feel like castoffs, who fear they've screwed up their lives, have found the shelter of a huge rock in Jesus Christ. They can finally come home.

This is the time in your life to let yourself get to know him. He can be found primarily in prayer and in the books of Matthew, Mark, Luke, and John in your Bible. There he walks the pages as God who came to earth as a man. Getting to know him is mostly about letting him in—letting ourselves be loved by him and giving over to him the things that fascinated us while they stole our very life, offering us no true sweetness and no real joy.

It is in simply *being* with him that we are restored and made whole. He is jealous for your love. His purifying gaze will heal even as it penetrates your soul. He is True North, the one who resets your inner compass such that when a man comes along who even remotely resembles him, you will know.

Questions for Discussion and Reflection

1. How would you describe the men to whom you have been attracted? What is good about it, and what differences would you like to see in terms of where your compass has been set?

2. How has your experience with the first man in your life—your father—affected your expectations of men or the way you relate to men?

3. What do you value and appreciate in a friendship with a man?

4. How do you think your relationship with a man might be different if the experience of being loved by God was more real to you?

5. When are you most tempted to develop an attitude of viewing men as expendable?

6. Suppose you took a break from relationships with men and devoted the time to your relationship with God. What would you want to ask God for during this season? What do you long to experience with him?

10

Giving Yourself Away

Sexuality is not simply about finding a lover or even finding a friend. It is about overcoming separateness by giving life and blessing it.

he movie *Antwone Fisher*, which told of an enlisted seaman's search for his real family, caught the public eye soon after its release. Antwone's tragic flaw is a boatload of anger that stems from an abusive childhood and causes him to use his fists to speak his mind. The movie also storyboards the double message our culture sends regarding sex, for the brawl that finally lands Antwone in jail is sparked by an insult one of his shipmates hurls his way in a bar during shore leave. He dares to call Antwone "a virgin." His dark secret is exposed, and he is humiliated. Now everyone knows—Antwone is twenty-five years old and has never been with a woman.

Antwone's psychiatrist (played by Denzel Washington) treats Antwone's virginity as evidence of his lack of mental health, a condition in need of curing. When Antwone finally sleeps with his girlfriend, Denzel congratulates him as though he has just graduated from college.

What a turn of events that something as valuable as virginity could take on the aura of a taboo. The strange twist in a sexualized culture like ours is that those who exercise restraint feel like the deviant ones, the odd ducks. Yet this is where we are. What does it mean when you choose sexual freedom in the form of boundaries that leave the richest physical experience between a man and a woman to marriage? Moreover, how do you shut the door on sex without shutting down as a woman?

These are the questions that women who remain single for a number of years grapple with—and I confess that I listen with more than a little humility when they talk. I recognize that I have not slept alone in quite some time. And I would be the first to agree that sex itself is pretty good stuff. A woman's choice to forgo an active sexual life and to live in celibacy for the sake of her own freedom and sanity is no small thing.

I am grateful, though, for the earlier experience of pulling back from the edge sexually. I know what it is to feel alone and OK walking out into the world unattached to any man. It is so different to experience a relationship, then, that grows out of friendship and respect that has not been catapulted forward via the sexual. It places the decision to marry on much firmer footing. You know this man in so many varied ways that knowing him sexually is just one more piece—albeit a very good one. I count it as one of the great undeserved graces of my life to have a sexual bond with my husband rooted so deeply in trust.

Having said this, though, let me share some thoughts and insights that have come from helping single women navigate relationships once a sexually pure lifestyle becomes their intent.

Awakening love in the wrong context means that appetite has to be lulled back to sleep.

Courage is required. Sex is much like any other physical appetite. Once you've tasted chocolate, you tend to want more. If you have grown accustomed to running a couple of miles a day, your body feels like it is missing something if you aren't out there pounding the pavement. And if sex has been an ongoing part of your life and a pleasurable one, it takes real courage to let go of this experience of intimacy for the time being, until God returns it to you in its rightful form. That's why Solomon, in the one book of the Bible devoted to romance and sex, repeats this wise caution three times, "Daughters of Jerusalem, I charge you: Do not arouse or awaken love until it so desires."[1]

There is a time to awaken love, God says. And conversely, awakening love in the wrong context means that appetite has to be lulled back to sleep.

Some feel that one reason God has enabled such a richness in praise and worship music in our day is to provide a vehicle that can carry us into his presence, where a greater love envelops us.[2] God knew we would need a way to come to him by which lesser passions could be swallowed up by a greater passion. In letting go of physical intimacy, we are deepening our intimacy with him and trusting his heart to restore our hope for a future infinitely better than we could create by our own devices. As Lisa Bevere writes, "Holiness is not God asking us to be 'good'; it is an invitation to be 'His.' "[3] We belong to him. The best synonym for *holiness* is the word *freedom.*[*]

It takes time and commitment for sexual appetite to calm down. Thankfully, it won't leave in any permanent way. Sexual pleasure will be there waiting—waiting to be reawakened in a whole new context with a man and a future shared together. But the pull of the flesh is strong. That's why the biblical instruction is a simple one: Flee.[4] Run in another direction. Give yourself to the company of those who are actively pursuing God. This is the very opposite of the "going on a diet" mentality some associate with abstinence. Rather, the energy that would have been siphoned off in sex gets invested in other ways. Life opens up in different ways, like a smorgasbord of opportunities that leads to growth.

A change in motivation is necessary. When a woman's orientation to relationships starts to change and connection to a man is about everything except exchanging sexual favors, new questions emerge. Her sensitivities are awakened in other areas. She starts to see her own motivations more clearly.

A veterinarian in her late twenties helped me follow the way a woman's motivation in relationships can radically change once sexual games aren't the focus of attention. Cynthia claims that she never really saw how she used sex as a

---

[*] It is worth noting that the words *healthy* and *holy* come from the same Anglo-Saxon root *halig*.

way to guarantee relationship — until sex wasn't in the picture. At first she felt insecure around a man. Being sexually intimate had been a way to feel in control. Her needs for closeness and male affirmation had been met in sexual ways, and her ego received a consistent stroke — even though she hated the way things fell apart later.

Forgoing a sexual relationship opened her eyes to the sheer selfishness governing her life with men. She had lived in relationships like any good consumer, asking herself, "What am I getting? What's in this for me? How can I get this guy to give me what I need?" Cynthia feels that celibacy is what led her to her first taste of real freedom with men. "I discovered the pleasure of being with a guy without trying to manipulate his affection," she explains. "I have learned, as a woman, how to enjoy a man without trying to hook him."

SHUTTING THE DOOR
WITHOUT SHUTTING DOWN

Those of us who advocate the fullest of sexual expression within the narrowest of constraints — the marriage relationship — know that we are walking a fine line. Messages of "just say no to sex" are sometimes said or heard with such negativity that sexuality itself gets covered in shame. All that is feminine, beautiful, and attractive gets locked down tight, stuffed in a back closet somewhere, and labeled "bad." When this happens in a woman's life, it must grieve the heart of God. Nothing on the planet is more essentially our birthright than our sexuality — the pleasure and beauty of being female.

Living as a woman with a sexually pure lifestyle without

unsexing yourself backs quickly into the larger canvas of what it means to be sexual—and what it means to be female. The issue is deeper than having sex or not having sex. The real questions are ones most of us face at one time or another: What do we do with unmet desire? How is the expression of myself as a woman experienced in a larger sense than sex itself?

Friends who are single and have wrestled with these questions well and deeply have provided real insight into both. They refuse to let our culture reduce their femaleness to what they provide sexually. One friend in particular tells a funny, sad story to which many women relate:

> One day when I was teaching high school English (fifth period—I shall never forget this class), I was in a particularly foul mood. Truly, that class could have put a veteran master teacher in a foul mood, but it was particularly tortuous for me, a twenty-five-year-old brand-new teacher. I do not remember the exact sequence of events, but I know it culminated with a kid I'll call Jimmy (greasy, long hair, repeating tenth grade, wearing tight, skinny jeans) who stood up and yelled, "I know what Miss Gillam's problem is: She ain't gettin' any!"
>
> Amazingly, the class went absolutely silent— something they never did. His words shocked even them. Finally, Misty, a tough cookie in her own right, but one who'd come over to my side, said, "Shut up, Jimmy. Sit down."

I took one moment to assess the situation, decided Misty's words, still echoing, were enough, and moved forward as if nothing had happened. But it took a whole lot longer to shake it off inside.

Was that my problem—I just wasn't gettin' any?[5]

What a haunting question! My friend admits there are moments when, like anyone, she longs for "warm flesh against warm flesh," the simple human comfort of physical touch. On a bad day, she struggles with the fear that she'll wake up one day shriveled, living with a bunch of cats and wearing a beige cardigan as she rocks in her favorite chair. This question of gettin' some or not gettin' some is a live issue to her. It has driven her past the question of sex into the real nature of sexuality itself.

Amazingly enough, excellent insight into the larger question of sexuality comes through the writings of a Catholic priest named Ronald Rolheiser. What he writes about sexuality *in the absence of a sexual relationship* far outweighs the wisdom of those who do not sleep alone. Rolheiser begins at the place of noting that the word *sex* means "to cut off" or "to sever." Sexuality, then, speaks to our awareness from birth of being disconnected from the whole—lonely, cut off, severed from others.[6] Thus, in both the sexual act and in our sexuality, our desire is to reconnect—to overcome our incompleteness.

Our culture is fixated on the act of sex, and as a result, we miss the larger picture of sexuality. As great as sex itself is, sexuality is something more. It is this all-encompassing energy inside us that drives us out into the world in a creative, life-giving way. It moves us toward unity and consummation with that which is beyond us.

> *Our culture is fixated on the act of sex, and as a result, we miss the larger picture of sexuality.*

The accusation that my friend's irritability was the result of "not getting any" led her into a deeper search for what her sexuality was about. She concluded, paradoxically, that what keeps men and women alive as sexual beings grows out of what they are giving of themselves. It's not what a person is getting or not getting that matters; it's what he or she is *giving*. By this truer standard, for example, even Mother Teresa could be called an erotic woman. She grew wrinkled and old, to be sure—but she did not dry up. In the giving of herself, she was one of the most alive women of her time. As Rolheiser explains, "A mature sexuality is when a person looks at what he or she has helped create, swells in a delight that breaks the prison of his or her selfishness, and feels as God feels when God looks at creation."[7]

The path through the forest, as my friend has found, comes out of the paradox of owning her desire without narrowing the expression of her femaleness to sex. She has learned to let herself enjoy the fact that men find her attractive—without having to go there. She is not running in place, keeping life on hold until she is married. She has found that it is useless to try to fulfill sexual hunger in illicit ways. They do not satisfy. The hole in her soul only gets larger. Even though she has some genuine unmet needs, she feels that wrestling with the crucible of sexuality has not undone her as a woman; rather, it has made her.

COMING ALIVE

We live in a chaotic time in which the old road maps to being a man or a woman don't seem to work. The important cues are still there, hidden in our members, but it takes longer and we work harder to find the way. Men and women no longer marry upon college graduation, like clocks programmed to strike twelve at the same time. Many more of us are single — some by choice, many unintentionally. The right man just has not come along yet.

In the wake of unmet desire, the woman who "plays by the rules" sexually and yet remains single can sometimes feel resentful, as though she has not seen the payoff. Even worse is the woman who interprets her singleness as punishment for some era of promiscuity in her past. Both of these responses painfully miss the larger cultural picture of what is happening in our day. Neither fits the truth of the matter. Finding a man is not a reward that comes to virtuous women necessarily — or to women who have resolved all of their personal issues. If that were the case, none of us would be married.

I talked with a woman recently who married at thirty-eight and had her first child at forty. She had wanted to be married much sooner. "Now I look back," she says, "on the rich experiences I had when I was single — the travel and friends, the hobbies I pursued, the luxury of uninterrupted time with God — and I am so grateful for those years I kept praying to get past. I wouldn't want anything different."

The truth is that every woman I know, myself included, lives with some very real unmet needs in her life — ones that tug at her heart daily. It may be childlessness, a dead-end career, a difficult marriage, or a host of other open wounds—but trust me, it's there. No one comes through this life unscathed.

All of us face the same essential choice in life. We can shut down inside, clamp off the pain of unmet desire, and live in a small place where we feel almost nothing. Plenty of women make this choice, often subconsciously. It feels safer than taking the risks that "having a life" entails, but it is really a form of dying on the vine.

To move courageously, you have to hold on to hope, knowing there are no guarantees how your life story will read. You hold on to hope, and you *trust* that God has a better script for your life than you could write on your own. Married or not, childless or with a house full of little feet, at the top of your field or amazingly average—God's blessing is on your life because the gospel of Jesus is real and true. And if it is true indeed, then you refuse to dull your heart, because being half alive is not what you were made for. You choose to live from the inside out, offering yourself in a hundred good ways to the people God brings your way.

The second path is harder. Anyone will tell you this in a heartbeat. But it leads to a place worth going, and this makes all the difference. To live in the rarer air of the in-between—neither shutting down desire nor demanding it be fulfilled in a particular way—is your own heart's journey in what it means to trust God with your life. The disease to be feared is not, as our culture claims, that somehow we won't "get any." The real fear is that you and I will go through life holding back the life God has put in us, playing it safe. We'll miss "giving it."

The pain of unmet desire can actually enlarge our hearts. The more we let ourselves long for life, even though it brings the ache of incompleteness, the more we are actually able to savor the joy that comes our way. This paradox surprises me on a daily basis. More and more, I recognize this kind of pain for what it is—a ticket to becoming a woman so thoroughly alive that she is afraid of almost nothing.

Questions for Discussion and Reflection

1. What is the challenge of walking out into the world alone and unattached to a man?

2. How do you respond to the thought that your sexuality is the energy that drives you out into the world in a creative, life-giving way?

3. In what way does sexuality break the prison of our selfishness? What might this look like in your life?

4. How might living with a desire that has not yet been fulfilled be something that embodies hope, not just disappointment?

5. How would leaning in the direction of hope affect your life?

11

The Good Relationship

Human beings always cast ahead of themselves into the morrow, and they bring along with themselves their yesterdays. The self does not fully give itself—however fervent the act—if it withholds the future.

–William F. May

When Lynn's friend wanted to set her up with a guy named Jeff Mason, Lynn just rolled her eyes. She knew Jeff from a distance, and he wasn't her type, plain and simple. So Lynn played it safe—she agreed to meet Jeff for a cup of coffee.

The problem was that she had a much better time with Jeff than she expected.

They talked like old friends. She had more fun, just plain fun, than she'd had with any guy she could remember. That was the other part of the problem—there had been a good many guys before Jeff.

Lynn had grown up as "the responsible child" in a family with six children and a mom who worked two jobs trying to make ends meet. The first guy she slept with was a man she met in a bar the summer she turned nineteen. The attention he showed her was like candy to a starving kid. Six months later, she felt stung as she watched him do the same number on another girl—at the same bar, no less. Soon after, she moved out of state, and in her newfound independence, she had a number of one-night stands that pain her to recall. Her career took off, and by age twenty-six, she met a man she thought she could build a life with. Two years into their marriage, he cheated on her.

All this time, Lynn was vaguely aware of God as though he were a rather imposing figure standing mute on the edge of her consciousness. But there was nothing that could be called a relationship. "Don't count on anyone but yourself" was the creed her mother had taught her. Lynn didn't need anyone. She most surely didn't need God.

After Lynn's divorce, she started dating a man who seemed more promising. While they lived together, he took her to church. Within a few months, Lynn gave her life to Christ, though she admits she went home and cried for three days, suddenly awake to the scary realization that fundamentally she was divorced and alone and living with a man. The future did not look good. She only knew one way to do life— her way—and she knew only one way to relate to a man. None of it had made her happy, but she had no idea how to do things differently.

Slowly, Lynn began to grow spiritually, drawn by the love of Christ. God put his finger on areas of her past she needed to let go of, one by one—and promiscuity with a man was the last major one Lynn relinquished. When yet another man cheated on her, Lynn realized she needed a sabbatical from relationships. By now she was thirty-five years old. "For six months God and I dated exclusively," Lynn explains. "For the first time in my life I was content and happy with myself. It was amazing."

Then she had coffee with Jeff. And then, as these things go, she had another cup. And another. Lynn admits that for a while she didn't know what to do with a man who treated her so well. It was a brand-new sensation to feel respected—like this guy was genuinely interested in *her*, with no angles. Jeff could see beyond the mess she had made. He brought out the best in her. The analogy Lynn uses is that, before Jeff, she had a "love box" filled with all the false ways she had learned to feel loved by a man. Jeff dumped everything out of the box and began to fill it with something much purer—something a lot more like the love of God.

Lynn and Jeff began to see each other regularly, but they credit a friend with moving their relationship to a new level. "So," the friend asked Jeff, "are you just dating or are you actually courting Lynn?"

"What's courting?" Jeff asked in all innocence. Being Australian by birth, Jeff thought this might be another American invention.

"Oh, you know," the friend replied. Then she offered an unconventional means of romantic involvement. "Courting is when you give a woman a quarter each time you see her, and the great fun is to see where she finds it. You *court her* with *quarters*."

Thus began a romantic surprise that came hidden in nearly every date. Lynn might find a quarter in her shoe, or under her dinner plate, or waiting for her on a chair. She never knew. What she did know was that every time she found a quarter, Jeff had thought about her. Something wonderful was starting to happen between them. On the evening Jeff asked Lynn to marry him, he began by giving her a quarter he had framed. The inscription read, "This is the last quarter I hope to give you." They married six months later.

Lynn and Jeff are quick to say that deciding to save physical intimacy until they were married was particularly hard because "they'd been there" with others. For Lynn especially, sex meant the deep reassurance that she was loved. She remembers praying one morning early in their courting and words forming in her brain as clear as though she had heard them out loud: *Do ... not ... sleep ... with ... this ... man.* God could not have made it clearer to her that *this* relationship was to be different from all the others. She and Jeff made a vow together to wait until they were married—a pledge that sent Jeff running out the door on occasion. But this same vow also led to a sweet season of romance and playfulness. "It was a whole new kind of freedom," Lynn says. "I felt loved and respected and honored in the purest sense."

Allowing physical intimacy to follow marriage rather than precede it feels like an investment that Lynn and Jeff are still cashing in on. "To be sure, I wish Jeff had been the only man I'd been with," Lynn says. "But the struggle and commitment to wait have built a real solidity in our relationship."

She notes that when they argue and the air gets tense, it never crosses her mind that Jeff will leave. Something very strong has been forged between them.

Lynn and Jeff have been married four years now. They are parents of a daughter almost two years old. "Sometimes when I look into my daughter's eyes," Lynn explains, "I am bowled over by the mercy of God."

BUILDING A RELATIONSHIP ON TRUST

In a day when the signals between men and women are not so clear, it is hard to tell when you have come upon a special connection with a man. "Is he a keeper?" as the expression goes. As Lynn's story suggests, sometimes a man you might never expect can turn out to be the love of your life.

But how would you know? A man does not come with a tag that says, "Trust me. I won't let you down." There is no machine that takes an X-ray of the heart. Oh, people will tell you that a good relationship means that two people have common interests and similar values. They will ask you if, indeed, you are physically attracted to this guy (in other words, he doesn't just seem like a good brother). A paycheck is always nice. The hope of future paychecks is especially nice. He may have the blue eyes you always dreamed of and the manners your mother thinks are indispensable in a man. You may feel like the luckiest woman alive when you're with him. But none of these things are enough. And all of it put together does not get at the elusive quality that all good relationships have in common.

In other words, you can't build anything with a man for the long haul that is not infused, through and through, with *trust*. Trust is the root from which love flowers and continues to bloom. How you answer the question "Can I trust this man?" will determine whether you feel you can give your heart in any significant way.

> Trust is the root from which love flowers and continues to bloom.

I knew I could trust the man I married—largely because of the way we met. We were both part of a summer program in which we worked at various jobs in Birmingham, Alabama, and then did activities and Bible studies in the evening. I met Stacy in a car pool headed out to a particular section of the city each day. Only this was one of the quieter guys I'd ever been around. I couldn't really engage him in conversation.

One day, though, someone asked him about racquetball. He was an authority on the subject because he played eight hours a day in the army, when he managed their facilities. Suddenly, he started to ask me what kind of racket I preferred and what size court I liked. I made up my answers. I just invented them out of thin air. I was just so amazed that he asked me a question. As soon as I opened the door, the thought struck me: I'm going to have to admit to this guy that I lied to him.

The next morning I confessed, a bit sheepishly, that I'd never played racquetball in my life. He smiled. He accepted my apology and began to talk a lot more freely. Our friendship took off from that point. The X-ray of his character I'd been given at the beginning proved consistent as I got to know him. He was a man of integrity who had enough grace to handle life—and to handle me.

I'm not advocating that you lie to a guy in order to prove his trustworthiness. And I realize that trust in relationship is a bit abstract and hard to explain. It's almost something you come to sense in your gut. For some time now, I have taken it upon myself to interview women on the question of how, exactly, they came to know they could trust the man they married. Or in the case of one single woman, I asked her how she separated the men she could take home to her father from the fish she threw back in the pond. The responses I received are worth a small book itself.

Does He Mean What He Says?

As simple as it sounds, a woman's most common response about a man they can trust is that he does what he says and says what he means. There is something quietly reassuring about a man who, when he tells you he'll call before dinner, actually picks up the phone and who, when he says he'll come by tomorrow night, actually shows up—or if he doesn't, he has a good explanation.

Watch for a basic congruence between words and feelings and actions. For example, a man says he thinks you are the best thing since sliced bread. You hear the words, and he may be looking deeply into your eyes when he says them, but do his actions match his words? Does he treat you like a man would treat a woman he really cared for? You don't want to make the mistake of loving a man so much that you overlook a big disconnect between what he says, what he seems to feel, and what he does. Those three need to line up pretty consistently.

Can This Man Be Wrong?

It is amazing how much strength is communicated through the quality of humility and especially the absence of an ego that requires continual feeding.

I once worked with a couple who had broken off their engagement shortly before the wedding. Within two weeks, the would-be groom knew he had made the mistake of his life. His wedding jitters had been little more, really, than an indicator of his need to grow up and take responsibility for loving a wonderful woman who had less of a pedigree than his family wanted. In the painful aftermath, he saw his mistake with crystal clarity. He did the hard work of deep personal change. He also put feet to his new understanding. With no one's prompting, he humbled himself enough to drive half a day to apologize to his ex-fiancée's parents and her family. This was his idea entirely — and a rather courageous one, since he knew he could meet with a door slammed on his nose. But when a man lets go of his pride, God gives him a kind of strength that is rooted in something larger than himself.

Later, his still ex-fiancée asked me, "Do you think I'd be the fool of the century to marry this man, given all we've been through?" A broken engagement had been a crushing disappointment for them, yet they were still very much in love.

It was a totally understandable question. Any woman would think twice. "I think you are asking a deeper question about whether you can trust this man," I replied. And then I encouraged her to weigh the amount of change she saw in the man she loved. Weigh, especially, the humility he displayed in taking responsibility for his immaturity. Does his humility lead her to a deeper trust?

It is amazing how much strength is communicated through the quality of humility.

You don't want to match up with a man who cannot admit he's wrong. Not in the rain and not on the train, as Dr. Seuss would say. His ego is too fragile to bear the thought. So whatever is wrong is someone else's fault. Run the other way, quick, because pretty soon, when bad things happen, it will be all *your* fault.

Does He Enjoy You?

More telling than whether a man is attracted to you or likes your family or admires your career is his enjoyment of you. Your intuitive sense of being enjoyed tells you whether you can trust him. Does this man just plain *like* you for who you are? Your adventuresome spirit may be an irritation to some, or your quietness may be misunderstood by many, but this man enjoys those kind of things about you. He sees in them real value and worth.

I asked a friend who is a great "idea woman," a lover of books, what sealed her affection for the man she married. Her response was telling. "He enjoyed my mind," she explained. He wasn't intimidated by her intelligence; he did not wish away her philosophical bent. She sensed she could trust this man with this crucial aspect of herself.

In the world of counseling, I have noticed that the question of "being enjoyed" is the one that most often brings a person to tears. "Does your father or your mother or a good friend or the man you married—or anyone on the planet—just plain enjoy you—as the unique and gifted, flawed and sometimes failing woman you are?" Ask that question, and be prepared to hand a woman a Kleenex. All of us long to feel that someone knows us deeply—and still loves us truly.

Being enjoyed by someone is very close to feeling really loved, perhaps as close as we get in this life. That's why we long to take pleasure in God and for him to take pleasure in us. And we will always want this from any man to whom we give our hearts.

Can He Take Risks for the Sake of Love?

To love a woman well requires that a man move out of himself and his own frame of reference. He steps outside himself into territory that feels as uncharted to him as anything Lewis and Clark faced when they ventured into the great Northwest. A genuine relationship with a woman to whom he commits himself, body and soul, is at once amazingly attractive and mildly terrifying—though, of course, few men would admit it. In a committed relationship, a man will have to do battle with feelings of inadequacy that appear regularly and out of nowhere. Taking risks for the sake of love tells you that a man is willing to engage in this battle.

Cecelia's story helps illustrate this. Of all the men Cecelia ever dated, Joel, an insurance broker with a love of all things aesthetic—poetry, paintings, books, classic architecture—was the one with whom she felt the most instantaneous connection. Dating Joel, however, was like dancing in tandem with a phantom. He would call her when he came to town, take her out for expensive dinners, and genuinely marvel at her intuitive ability to see into his soul. "You rattle me to my toes, and I love that," he would say on occasion. Then he would disappear into a haze of work and travel, punctuated with warm and cozy emails. But nothing more. He would get close and then get scared — and then drop off the face of the earth.

Cecelia hung in there because she just plain liked the guy that much. He was a wonderful man in many respects, but he was content to sample only. He would get right up to the edge of making a commitment to a relationship he clearly valued — and then he would back away from taking the actual risk that love entails. One night over coffee and dessert, after his declarations of how much he enjoyed an evening in her charming company, she pointed out this pattern.

"You know, I feel like a treasured bottle of wine to you. And you're content to simply pour a glass and then put the bottle back in the rack until next time," she said as gently and truthfully as she knew.

The color of hot pink slowly crept into Joel's cheeks. Her comment made him mad. It blew his cover. He had never had a woman call him on a pattern of toying with her — of reeling her in emotionally and then running away. If Joel simply could have owned his struggle to take a risk, he might well have overcome it. But he moved the other way — back into the world of pretense and pretending. When Joel called back a year later, he was still looking merely for a tasty sample. This time Cecelia declined.

A man you can trust will have a different response. He may sweat bullets inside at the thought of giving himself to one woman, one relationship. Love is full of take-your-breath-away risks. But when the time comes to do battle with his fear, he will face it and move through it and become stronger in the process. He will not just string you along.

THE MOST ESSENTIAL X-RAY

As I said earlier, we all wish for a machine that could X-ray a person's heart. It would make trust much easier. The Bible offers not an X-ray but a set of scales that weighs out the character of a man. It's like saying, "Don't move forward in a relationship where these red flags are present." If you do, you'll find yourself skating on ice too thin to support you. The basis for trust will not be there.

If you have even a passing acquaintance with the Bible, you will have heard of the Proverbs 31 woman. She represents the highest ideals a man could hope to find in any woman. What most of us miss are the first nine verses of chapter 31 that describe the man who is worthy of such a woman. Or you might say these verses describe the essential starting points of what will become solid character in a man. Three characteristics in particular are pointed out here in the form of a mother's advice to her son.

1. "Do not spend your strength on women, your vigor on those who ruin kings."[1] In other words, beware of the man who is a womanizer—who needs the constant attention of a woman in order to function well. Look out for the man whose sense of self is wrapped around some woman's ankles. Who can't be alone and without a relationship. Who measures himself by the gleam of approval he sees in her

eyes—whoever she is. This tendency in men is so common that the first admonition out of this wise mother's mouth is, "Don't spend your strength on women." Even great men are destroyed this way. A man who gives his heart to God first will be able to love and serve a woman without being dependent on her. He is standing on his own two feet because he knows what it is to bow his knee and his will before God.

2. "It is not for kings ... to drink wine, nor for rulers to crave beer, lest they drink ... and deprive all the oppressed of their rights."[2] This is the scale of addiction. You can't build a lasting relationship with a person who is controlled by substance, because the addiction will control you both. Even a "king" will neglect to do the one thing he is most responsible for—to tend to the needs of the poor and the oppressed. Brought into the realm of a relationship, this is saying that you can't hope for much from a man who is overcome from within. As anyone who has ever been in love with someone in the grip of addiction will attest, it's like trying to hug a shadow.

3. "Speak up for those who cannot speak for themselves, for the rights of all who are destitute. Speak up and judge fairly; defend the rights of the poor and needy."[3] This is the mother's one prescription, one positive teaching. She is telling her son something terribly important—how to use his strength as a man. He is to be a man for others, a man to make things happen for those his influence touches.

Have you known a man who is far enough along to realize his potential influence, who wants his life to have an impact on others for good and for a cause larger than his own self-interests? Such a man will someday become like a huge oak tree whose roots sink deep and who provides shade and sustenance for many people. He knows he was put on the planet for more than his own pleasure—and you are the one who will most feel the benefit of this.

This last teaching gives crucial direction in discerning the kind of man you want to join your life with for the long haul. Simply put, has he moved beyond himself? Is he able to invite you to join him in something larger than either of you?

REAL VULNERABILITY

So trust is the basis for a love that lasts and a relationship that can weather the storms of life. As Lynn and Jeff's story reveals, it takes time and a bit of a track record to know whether what you think you see in someone is truly there. (And it goes without saying that what you would hope to see in another, you need to be in the process of actually becoming.) Personally, I'm in favor of a good many cups of coffee—maybe enough to support one local Starbucks near you.

What is happening as two people become a couple is like a prolonged card game—it takes a while to share your cards with each other. You each have in your hand a big deck full of past, present, and future cards. This deck includes a lot of interesting stuff. Like how you felt about going to a new high school your senior year and where you have been hurt and what scares you at 3:00 a.m. in the dark. Some of those cards have to do with the things you love and the experiences you hope never to repeat.

You will know that you love a man when you feel safe with him, even though the worst is known.

Some cast way into the future—the hopes and dreams you may only be beginning to admit to yourself. A few cards are tattered and frayed and probably hidden behind other ones you think are prettier. At some point in this fascinating interchange that takes place over weeks and months—maybe a few years—all the cards you know in your hand (some you don't know yet) need to be laid on the table. The good, the bad, and the "wish it had never happened."

This is the picture of vulnerability, which is the emotional fuel that empowers trust. The root of the word *vulnerability* is worth noting. It means "able to be wounded." It is the opposite of self-protection and the feeling that you always have to put your very best self forward. In the beginning of a relationship, the only self we can offer is our "best self," the one that has been most applauded in our past—our dazzling intellect, our stunning good looks, our deep spirituality. But it must go further. It must move into the places that feel more vulnerable. We may be met, not with applause and approval, but with the stale taste of rejection. That's the risk.

You will know that you love a man when you feel safe with him, even though the worst is known. And you will feel that you can trust each other when you sense that the best God has put in you is celebrated and truly enjoyed.

Vulnerability of the heart is always supposed to precede, by a long shot, vulnerability of the body, which is another euphemism for sex. It was such a gift to Lynn and Jeff, for instance, that sex was not allowed to preempt this far more intricate dance of getting to know each other. Sex didn't take over the card game.

It is a strange irony that sometimes it is less vulnerable

to be sexually involved—to be two strangers in the night—than it is to share your life and your heart with someone. Real vulnerability followed by genuine commitment to a person make sexual intimacy one of the best joys on earth. This sort of joy is simply not possible in a relationship that is not for keeps. As the opening quote by William May explains, we don't give ourselves to another fully if the future is withheld.

In the final analysis, a good relationship is not about the absence of vice. The celibacy of dating or courting or getting to know someone—all the precursors to marriage—is meant to clear out the space for the really important stuff to grow and flourish. You are planting a garden meant to last a lifetime. You are investing in a relationship that has to be nurtured and tended to all your days. In a good relationship, celibacy makes room for the practice of showing respect and honor to another. The self-giving allows the two of you to be better together than you could ever be apart.

Seen from certain angles, this coming together of two people can look like loss and subtraction, as though the giving of oneself is a kind of death. Perhaps in some ways it is. But it is death that also leads to the experience of personal resurrection. In this union of two people, body and soul, the sum is truly greater than the parts—and the individuals themselves become somehow more of who they truly are. In marriage there is a hint of something only God could dream up, something bigger than the two of you combined. Or as Frederick Buechner explains:

By all the laws of both logic and simple arithmetic, to give yourself away in love to another would seem to mean that you end up with less of yourself left than you had to begin with. But the miracle is that just the reverse is true, logic and arithmetic go hang. To give yourself away in love to somebody else … is to become for the first time yourself fully. To live not just for yourself alone anymore but for another self to whom you swear to be true—plight your troth to, your truth to—is in a new way to come fully alive.[4]

Questions for Discussion and Reflection

1. Think about the men you have known. What has been true of the ones you felt you could trust?

2. How much are the traits of humility, courage, freedom from addiction, and living for something larger than yourself a part of your life? Which of those do you most want to see growth in—and why?

3. When have you felt enjoyed by a man for who you are, and how would you describe the experience? What kind of impact did it have on you?

4. When you think of genuine vulnerability with someone, which word most describes your gut response? Why?
    - fear
    - longing

- mistrust
- joy
- shame

5. In terms of what you felt and understood as you read this chapter, how would you evaluate any relationship you might currently have with a man?

12

The Making of a Man

Most men want the maiden without any sort of cost to themselves.

JOHN ELDREDGE

For many a man, the most terrifying thing he can imagine is making a commitment to an equal, honest, intimate relationship with a woman.

DR. FRANK PITTMAN

Our discussion of sexuality would be incomplete without looking at the question from a man's vantage point. From all observations, it would appear to be a great time to be a guy. Sex has never been more readily available. And not just sex with one woman whom a man has to jump through hoops to please, but sex with a variety of women who may ask little of him at all. You would think men would be high-fiving each other on every street corner.

The age-old, acquired skill of learning how to court a

woman—to woo and romance her with no guarantee of anything in return—has nearly disappeared from the scene. Its loss
leaves an unnamed ache in all of us. Courting a woman is an
ancient rite of passage that helped turn a boy into a man you
could lean on, expect something of, and trust with your life.
We are all—men and women—suffering for the lack thereof.

When I talk to young women, I often find they feel a tad
guilty at the thought of denying sexual favor in its many and
varied forms to a man. Maybe it's just too hard on him to
expect that kind of restraint. And of course, there is always
the fear that he'll turn elsewhere for sexual intimacy. Such
guilt and fear, though, reveal how little most women understand about the way men come to be real men—and the
unrivaled role we play in this process.

GROWING UP MALE

When Ted looks back on his twenties, he sees how lost he was
in terms of relating to women. His immigrant father was a
man with a quick temper who didn't know much about the
tender parts of love. "Having a girlfriend was about making
myself feel good," Ted admits, a tad sheepishly. "If this woman
could make me happy, I was in the relationship. And if she
couldn't, it was over. Most of my twenties was about *me*."

Ted also admits that he struggled with Internet porn for
a few years. The fantasy of a woman who seemed to offer
an unending supply of affection hooked him. This screen-
sized woman wanted him, and she never, ever made him
feel rejected. It was so easy—too easy. Pornography sapped
him of his spiritual strength, turning his relationship with

God into a pile of mush that left him going through life in a lethargic, unmotivated haze. He felt like a man trying to climb a rocky mountain on stilts.

Knowing that he was now, at the age of thirty-five, engaged to a great woman, I asked how this transformation occurred. His response says a lot about the way a man moves from his own self-centeredness to being able to care for others—to love and shelter and lead them in the ways that men do best. "I eventually got tired of feeling ensnared by these images of women while being powerless to actually relate to one of them well. Honestly, a real longing for holiness came into my life. I wanted, more than anything, to be a man of integrity before God. And I began to ask—beg—God for my freedom."

Ted gained this freedom bit by solid bit and found in the process that his passion was dammed up into a reservoir of courage and initiative that enlivened every part of his life. His career took off. His mental fog cleared. "A verse in Proverbs describes what happened in my life," Ted says, going on to quote how the wicked person flees in the face of challenge but the righteous man is "as bold as a lion."[1] Ted began to experience this boldness. He had the strength to tackle things that had easily defeated him before.

Within a year or so, Ted met an interesting woman, and what caught his attention was the change in his own heart. "When I met Kristy," he says, "I had an overwhelming desire to love this woman well. I remember thinking how different it felt—to want to love and serve and give to a woman."

Contrary to other accounts, I am convinced there are good numbers of Teds out there, men who would echo his words. And more than anything, they need women in their lives who insist that they offer nothing less than they are capable of offering. Notice Ted's words: *want to love and serve and give to a woman.*

Ted's life is a window into the struggle of growing up male in our culture. For years now, men have felt the sting of shame attached to their masculinity — as though their maleness badly needed to be domesticated. Classic male traits are often treated these days as pathology to be cured. Boys are too active in class, so we give them Adderal. They play with guns, and we call them aggressive. They are big and loud and competitive, and it's a problem to be solved. Only lust is allowable, even expected of a true red-blooded male. As long as rape and pillage are not part of the picture, simple lust is seen as masculine — desired and highly prized. For many men, it is the only way they know to feel like a man.

A man's struggle here is crucial to understand. His masculinity is not a given to him. It is, in fact, much harder to feel secure in his maleness than it is for a woman to feel validated as a woman. "Do I have what it takes? Am I man enough?" These are the kinds of questions a man brings into any arena he enters — athletic competition, the corner office, the bedroom, or the battlefield. Can he meet the challenge? Being a man is more like a prize to be won, to be fought for in "small battles with honor" and proving oneself.[2]

AVOIDING THE EASIEST ROUTE

I offer these insights as backdrop to the discussion of how celibacy outside of marriage is actually the making of a man.

The easiest and surest way to feel like a man is to have sex. It is the quickest feedback loop, a deep physical dose of masculine validation. The experience of sexual virility is so potent for a guy that his lifelong temptation is to turn it into a god and to make the woman the center of his existence rather than a person in her own right and his partner.

Have you ever had a man try to make you the sun in his universe? It feels pretty good for a while—but only for a while. Then it starts to grow old because too much is hanging on you. Your words are too important, your presence too necessary. As John Eldredge notes in *Wild at Heart*, most women would prefer to accompany a man on the adventure of life; they do not want to be the adventure itself.[3]

When a man gets his sexuality confused with his soul, his actual self, he succumbs to what poet Robert Bly called "the myth of the Golden-Haired Woman."[4] Somewhere out there is a woman larger than life, the perfect soul mate, whose love and affection will make him a man. Think of all the movies built around this theme! Until he can break through this mirage, no ordinary woman will ever be enough. He will move from woman to woman,

> *The experience of sexual virility is so potent for a guy that his lifelong temptation is to turn it into a god.*

girlfriend to girlfriend, captured by the myth that the next woman can bestow the ultimate validation of himself as a man. Bly describes the illusion:

> He sees a woman across the room, knows immediately that it is "She." He drops the relationship he has, pursues her, feels wild excitement, passion, beating heart,

obsession. After a few months, everything collapses; she becomes an ordinary woman. He is confused and puzzled. Then he sees once more a radiant face across the room, and the old certainty comes again.[5]

It's as though, in some way, every man remembers Eve. As Eldredge puts it, "We are haunted by her. And somehow we believe that if we could find her, get her back, then we'd also recover with her our own lost masculinity."[6] This is the longing that fuels the myth for a man.

The problem comes when a man brings his quest for validation to you—or to any woman. Sexual intimacy is the easiest and quickest route he knows. But to go there is only to deepen the illusion that a woman's love is the salve of his soul. It is not. Femininity can never confer masculinity. He must find his own rootedness as a man in the One who made him and in the company of other men. As Eldredge states, "The masculine journey always takes a man *away* from the woman, in order that he may come back to her with his question answered. A man does not go to a woman to get his strength; he goes to her to *offer* it."[7]

What a fundamental shift! It is so different to have a man approach you out of the desire to offer his strength to you. He is free to look out for your interests as well as his own. And if he is really concerned about you, the last thing he wants to do is jeopardize your sexual integrity.

Once in the early days of knowing my husband, Stacy, when we were just two friends riding in a car pool to work in Birmingham, another guy (in the same car pool) touched me in a subtle but oddly inappropriate way. I shrugged it off as a fluke moment. Without a word from me, Stacy took the initiative to pull this guy aside later and talk to him. "What were you thinking? Didn't you realize the way you touched Paula was a bit off?" he asked. I was stunned. I had never had a man fight for my honor. And it felt surprisingly good.

When a man is not dependent on you for validation, he sees you differently. You are not the mirror of his worth. Your affection is not the ego stroke he rests on. He does not feel required to keep you happy or to make your life a bed of roses so that his life will be one. He loves you because this is what he was made to do—this is what a real man does. The joy comes, as Ted said, in being able to offer himself.

WHAT CELIBACY DOES FOR A MAN

Allowing a man to enjoy sexual favor without risking real commitment in marriage invites him to remain a boy inside. A recent national survey to discover why men won't commit to marriage as easily these days illustrates well how promiscuity permits men to get stuck as perpetual adolescents. These are the top reasons men gave for preferring to cohabit with a romantic partner—and why, if women will let them, they prefer to audition for marriage rather than take the manly leap.[8]

- They had the convenience of a regular sex partner they did not have to search for—she was just there waiting.
- There was someone to take care of the house and the dog when he was away.

- He felt "less answerable to a partner"; he could come and go as he pleased.
- His financial assets were better protected.
- A live-in girlfriend was his "best option for now," allowing him time to look for the ideal soul mate.

Do you hear the self-centeredness in these reasons men gave for preferring cohabitation to marriage? (Certainly, mere logic does not favor cohabitation as a preview to marriage, as the marriages that emerge from living together are less likely to succeed.) Sexual favor before marriage simply stunts the growth of boys into real men who can shoulder the responsibility of others because they have moved outside the narrow confines of their own immediate needs.

The promiscuous man knows deep down that his strength is being dissipated.

In the best of ways, celibacy causes the damming up of a man's strength and vitality. It forces him to deal with himself. He has to do battle with his sexuality, to ride it like a wild stallion until its power is harnessed and under his control. Then he gets the great gift of being able to use his sexuality for a larger purpose. This is the reasoning behind the verse often quoted in this regard: "For this is the will of God, your sanctification; that is, that you abstain from sexual immorality; that each of you know how to possess his own vessel in sanctification and honor, not in lustful passion."[9]

Don't you love that phrase—"to possess his own vessel"? (Try that on the next man who comes on to you: "Honey, you just need to possess your own vessel.") However antiquated the words, the imagery is important. Possessing one's own vessel speaks of a man's need to be the captain of his own ship if he ever intends to sail the high seas or carry the lives and cargo of others with him.

While it is true that men who can find a good supply of women to bed seem to swagger with confidence, their inner lives are another thing altogether. The promiscuous man knows deep down that his strength is being dissipated. He is Samson with his hair cut. His virility is confined to the four corners of a bed when it is meant, quite literally, to change the world.

Having to actually court a woman is something no man should be allowed to miss. Does it strike you what a gift it is to a guy when *he* has to be the one to pursue you? Men become men by doing battle with their fears, and pursuing a woman well is a process filled with man-sized risks. He must cross the floor to ask you to dance at age thirteen. He picks up the phone a few years later, braced for the sound of rejection or reception in your voice. On and on the dance goes, until one day he must gather the courage to stake his whole future on asking you to be his wife.

At every juncture, a man feels naked and fearfully exposed, braced for the turndown. But that's the nature of fear; it only subsides when you walk straight into it. To grow up inside, a man must get past his fear of Woman. For as we all know, we come to hate the things we fear. How can a man ever love you well if he is still so afraid of your rejection?

One man who built custom homes for a living explained to me how leaving the world of the sexually illicit helped him overcome his fears. He said, "I finally realized all this mingling and tingling kept me from actually feeling my need of a woman long enough to do something about it—like make an intentional, gutsy move toward one woman in particular." Indeed, making this move toward a woman-in-particular is the point. A man walks into the fire without the blanket of sexual affirmation around him. He does the thing a man is supposed to do: he pursues a woman to know her in this larger, fuller sense with absolutely no expectation that he will be rewarded with physical intimacy.

It is by such means that men become men.

GOD AND MEN

As a woman, I take my cues—which is to say that I learn a lot—by watching the way God addresses a man. I have already alluded to the straightforward instructions God gives a man about his sexuality: "Possess your own vessel ... in honor." Indeed, sexuality is the place God begins with a man. The first rite in the Jewish tradition is the act of circumcision, eight days after a boy's birth. A fascinating piece of history lies behind this requirement.

In the pagan culture that surrounded the Hebrew religion, male sexuality controlled the culture. In our language we would say, "It was a zoo." There were no boundaries. Sex and worship were joined. A man could worship his god by having sex with a temple prostitute. Homosexuality among Greek men was rampant. Indeed, a common expression was "A man for pleasure, a woman for babies." Women existed as objects of male gratification in whatever form. They were hardly more than chattel.

Follow with me the staggering intervention of God into this hedonistic world. God called the Hebrews to be his chosen people, and he drew a firm boundary around sexuality, corralling its powerful forces to the enjoyment of one man and one woman for a lifetime — a union from which new life comes in the form of children and grandchildren to care for. (Remember that a man could not be conscripted for the army during the first year of marriage because bringing pleasure to his wife was literally his job description.) While polygamy was rampant throughout the Old Testament, it was never God's intention, and it worked about as poorly as one would expect!

From a Hebrew boy's earliest days, then, his sexuality was marked by the touch of God on his life. In circumcision, his very flesh was cut. Daily he had the most graphic reminder possible that his sexuality was, first of all, a matter of covenant between God and himself. When he saw his own flesh, he remembered to whom he belonged.

The intervention of God into the lusts and desires of men not only allowed for the creation of culture; it established the basis by which a woman is to be cherished by a man. No longer could a man covet his neighbor's wife and get away with it. He could not enjoy a woman's sexual favor and then write her out a certificate of divorce when he found a younger version. A woman was to be honored as a lifelong partner. This "honoring" goes even further in the New Testament. There a husband is told that his wife is an equal partner sexually and that he is required to meet *her* sexual needs![10] He is called to love her sacrificially, "as Christ loved the church and gave himself up for her."[11] Furthermore, his prayers will tend to bounce off heaven if he does not live with his wife in an understanding way.[12]

Does this give you a better idea of the radical way in which God does business with a man and his sexuality?

A fascinating encounter between God and Job speaks volumes about how God views manhood. Job has lost everything—his children, his fortune, his health. He wishes he had never been born. He wonders how this has happened to him, a man who has lived a righteous life. His friends weigh in with their pathetic opinions. And then God speaks. Words of empathy and commiseration are not what God offers. Listen in on the particular kind of "comfort" God offers this tormented man:

> *"Who is this that darkens my counsel*
> *   with words without knowledge?*
> *Brace yourself like a man;*
> *   I will question you,*
> *   and you shall answer me.*
>
> *Where were you when I laid the earth's foundation?*
> *   Tell me, if you understand."*[13]

Does this sound harsh? God looks at Job in his misery and says the equivalent of, "Stand up and talk to me like a man." I believe God is here offering Job the greatest compliment he could give him. God is speaking to a man who thinks he has lost everything. And God tells him, in effect, that he has not lost the most essential thing of all. Job is invited to stand before the living God—as a man.

This is why it is a travesty for a man to rest his sense of self on you, a woman. Being a man is something God *bestows*—he gives innately as a good father would. No woman can take this away from a man unless he invests that kind of power and idolatry in her. And a woman cannot confer masculinity on a man no matter how many times she sleeps with him. All God allows either gender is to give witness to that which he has already done in the other.

THE FARMER TAKES A WIFE

Do you remember the nursery rhyme you sang as a child? "The farmer takes a wife, the farmer takes a wife, hi-ho, the derrio, the farmer takes a wife." It sounds like perhaps he has purchased her at the market, but the actual meaning behind the rhyme says something far more. It speaks of the huge responsibility a man takes on when he joins his life with a woman in marriage. I offer the story of a real couple by way of illustration.

John loved the summer he spent with Alice working in the mountains of North Carolina. She was willing to come to his hometown to serve tables at a local resort. Her grandmother lived conveniently nearby, so she had a place to stay. Nearly every night John and Alice found their own entertainment in the concerts and art shows and theatre venues that fill the warm nights of a vacation destination. It's not like they really needed "entertaining," for John was quite happy simply being with Alice. It mattered little to him what they did.

Their summer together was the climax to a year or so of

long-distance phone calls and occasional weekend visits. By
the time the summer ended, their relationship had come to
a fork in the road, and John felt this reality the most. As the
autumn leaves began to turn their first colors, an odd malaise
settled in on him. Where should this relationship go? Was
marriage the place where this was headed, and how did he
feel about it? Was he ready to take this on? John knew, in the
truest sense of the expression, the ball was in his court. He
and Alice could not continue to get closer and more attached
unless their relationship was going somewhere. That would
not be fair.

I watched John wrestle with this essentially male rite of
passage and recognized, perhaps for the first time, what steps
toward marriage feel like for a man. A man knows, deep in
his gut, that he is truly taking on the responsibility of other
lives in a whole new way. As one man shared insightfully, "A
woman dies to herself—her dreams and her agenda—when she has children. But a man does when he takes a wife."

> *It is important for us women to appreciate what love and courtship and marriage mean for a man—what he invests, the fears he must overcome, the joys he experiences.*

It is important for us women to appreciate what love and courtship and marriage mean for a man—what he invests, the fears he must overcome, the joys he experiences. Otherwise, we may miss this sweet death he dies. We may not
recognize the doors to relationship and deep connection that
we are privileged to open in him.

Perhaps you remember the true story, told in the movie

Anna and the King, about a widowed schoolteacher and her son who have come to teach the children of the king of Siam. She has a whole classroom of children to teach because the king has a number of concubines. He has no wife, but there are plenty of women in his life, since polygamy is the common practice of the monarchy. (What we see now in serial relationships with no lasting attachment isn't all that different.)

The king makes the mistake of falling in love with his children's widowed schoolteacher. He is angry with himself, for he has upset the order of his own kingdom. He is accustomed to having the affection of women who serve him at his beck and call. But he has never had a relationship with one—not until Anna. In a scene where the two of them are dancing outside his palace, looking out over the ocean, the king utters a line that could be echoed by men throughout the ages. He says, "I didn't know there was so much to be had in the love of one woman."

That's the secret you possess. You are capable of inviting a man into a relationship so deep and valuable that it is worth the reordering of his entire life. There is so much to be had in the love of one woman—there is so much to be had in your love. You have such a good gift to offer the right man that it must not be squandered. It means too much.

You are designed to usher a man through the door of his sexuality into another world relationally, one that will provide him the richest dividends of his life—children, family, deep connection to others, posterity. Finally, his sexuality will become fruitful in ways greater than he could have imagined.

In his real and lasting attachment to one woman, he sheds the empty freedom of his bachelor state. For you, he will leave behind his trivial pursuits. You are the prize, and your love is worth the death he must die.

Most of us women, when we know the worth of what we have to bring to a man, will guard it with our lives. It is the treasure God put in you. He himself cups his hands around it like a light that flickers in the darkness. Whatever has happened in your life — nevertheless, the light burns steadily on.

And even the darkness is not able to overcome it.

Questions for Discussion and Reflection

1. What kind of insight did this chapter give you into the particular challenges of growing up male?

2. Has a guy ever made you "too important" in his life? How did it make you feel?

3. Think, for a moment, of a relationship with a guy where he was trying to gain his validation from you. How did that feel and why? What kind of effect did it have on you?

4. How is it different (or how do you think it would be different) when a guy offers his strength to you?

5. How would you discern whether a man is indeed overcoming his own set of fears—regarding you, regarding life? What do you see as key to this?

6. What do you learn about men from the way God deals with them? How might this affect the way you relate to a man in a relationship?

Afterword

I hope you have found the material in this book helpful in your own journey. Confronting the questions and exploring the longings that lie at the root of your sexuality aren't easy tasks, but doing this can make such a difference in your life. Your sexuality touches every aspect of who you are. It has the potential to shape the way you think of yourself and how you relate to a man. And most especially, it is an amazingly powerful avenue by which you come to know God and to be known by him.

As you finish this book, I leave you with a verse I have come to love:

> *And let the beauty of the LORD our God be upon us,*
> *And establish the work of our hands for us;*
> *Yes, establish the work of our hands.*[1]

Appendix

A Brief Tour of What the Bible Has to Say about Sex and Sexuality

*H*aving thought about how themes of sexuality play out in our personal lives and in the culture around us, you can follow this theme through the Bible.

This section can be done gradually on your own. I recommend writing the insights that come to you on various passages in a journal so they have a chance to sink in deeply and come back to you later.

This section can also be done in the context of a small group, where you have the chance to hear how others react to a passage. You might want to read a chapter of *Sex and the Soul of a Woman* and also discuss a small section of Scripture, along with several questions provided to you about various passages. (They will not necessarily correlate, but by the time you finish both, you'll have a more complete picture of sexuality from a human and a biblical vantage point.)

Beginning at the Beginning

Every few years, I reread the account of God's creation of the original man and woman, Adam and Eve. I pretend I am watching a stage drama featuring God with Adam and Eve. And I ask God to show me something more of his heart, his original design for men and women. Every time—*every time*—I see things I hadn't seen before. Whenever I present these passages in a group setting, members of the group come up with insights that are brand-new, at least to me.

There is a world of truth that you see played out every single day in your life—in the lives of men and women you know—right out of the original drama of Adam and Eve. Enjoy these passages as they are meant to be savored, with wonder and humility. Ask God to show you his original intent for your life as a woman.

Genesis 1–2:17
Read this section and marvel at the grandeur of all God created. What was his purpose for humankind?

Genesis 2:18–25
Take more time here and watch the drama. What does this passage tell you about the needs of a man, the value of a woman, the beauty and innocence of the two of them together? What longings does this picture stir in you?

Genesis 3
This chapter describes relationships as we experience them now—not the way they were intended, but the reality of

how they actually are in this moment. It is a reminder of all we lost as a result of sin in the garden of Eden. But it's also the basis for hope in what we can experience in relationships—in small measure—as Christ redeems them.

Why would God make anything in the garden off-limits?

Try putting in your own words the lie that Eve swallowed about herself—and especially about God—when she ate from the tree. What shape does this same lie take in your life?

Where is Adam? What is his great omission in this story? What does he fail to do when God confronts him? How do we do the same thing with God and in relationships?

Look at this key line: "I was afraid because I was naked, so I hid myself." (Adam's words in 3:10) How do you and I replicate this same pattern in relationships? What does it cost us?

What does it say about God that he came seeking Adam after he ate from the tree?

Look at the specific consequences placed on Eve (women) and Adam (men). How do these consequences reveal something innate about each gender and the issues that drive us back to God in obedience and trust?

At a later point, read Genesis 1–3 again as you'd watch a drama. Ask yourself: What does this tell me about God, about men, about women? How does this apply to my life?

Ephesians 5:22–33

Flip over to the New Testament, to the classic instructions given to a man and woman in marriage. Notice that Paul refers back to Genesis. Think hard and creatively on this one: How do you see that these directives have the potential, as we follow them, to actually roll back some of the curse of the original fall of Adam and Eve?

What old aches are healed in some small measure?

Sex in the City: David and Bathsheba

What I love about the Bible is that it doesn't airbrush anyone. Here is sex outside the prescribed boundaries in detail and right out there for public display, committed by a major character, King David.

2 Samuel 11 and 12

Very simply, what caused David to be vulnerable to the ancient wrong of adultery? And what were the consequences for himself, for Bathsheba, for Uriah, for his son, for his household?

Psalm 51

What all do you see in this intimate moment of remorse as David talks to God about what he's done? What part of this psalm would most match the words inside of you? Why?

Incest and Lust

Again, nearly every human experience imaginable is found between the covers of the Bible. Amnon is David's son who forces himself sexually on his half sister, Tamar.

2 Samuel 13

What insight does this story give you into the nature of lust and its consequences? Why do you think Amnon hated Tamar as much as he had originally desired ("loved") her? What do you learn here that has bearing on other sins of lust, such as pornography or hooking up?

The Woman of His Nightmares

Solomon, the wisest man in the ancient world, had some astute thoughts about sex. His proverbs give a timeless take on the nature of seduction and the vulnerability of men.

Proverbs

Proverbs 5:1 – 6: How does this passage describe the seductive woman?

   Proverbs 5:21, 23; 6:26 – 35; 7:27 – 27: What are the consequences of getting involved with her? How have you seen these play out in a man's life?

   Proverbs 5:15 – 20: How is sexual desire meant to be fulfilled in marriage?

   Proverbs 7:6 – 27: What poor choices led to this man's affair?

Song of Songs

This is a book in the Bible that deserves to be savored in its entirety.

   Read it leisurely. Notice what happens in you as you read. How does it speak to the place in you that would somehow make sex or sexual desire something separate from God? God is not mentioned in this book — but he is present. What do you sense is his attitude toward sex?

   In the woman's last speech, she says, "My own vineyard is mine to give" (8:12). How is this insight key to future sexual intimacy with a husband, and what would it mean for you to make these your words?

A Heart Restored

Isaiah 61:1–3

When Jesus first had the opportunity to speak publicly in the temple, he spoke from this passage. What is God able to do in the places of our lives where we have known bondage and sorrow? Which phrase means the most to you? Why?

Hosea 2:14–17

This is God speaking, God who gives us a door of hope in the Valley of Achor (trouble). The God we come to know as a husband (Ishi) rather than someone who just controls us (owner). As you read this passage, what parts ignite a sense of hope in you? Why?

Jesus and Sex

We mostly know what Jesus thinks about the matter by the way he treated women who had a sexual past. That is, he did not condone. He did something far greater: he forgave, and he loved. Look at three individual women.

Luke 7:36–50

(The sinful woman is most likely a prostitute or a woman with an immoral sexual past.) How do you think this woman felt, weeping in a roomful of men? How can forgiveness transform someone to this extent?

John 4:1–42

How does Jesus treat this woman's past and her longings as they are revealed by the search for a man's love?

John 8: 1–11

Why did this woman remain behind after everyone left? How does Jesus deal with shame—her shame, my shame, your shame?

Paul and Sex

Paul's words about what is sexually permissible between men and women take on added weight when you realize the people he's writing to. Corinth was the cosmopolitan crossroads of its day, right at the center of trading between East and West, a potpourri of everyone from everywhere living there.

1 Corinthians 5

What does this passage say about immorality in the church and the modern notion of tolerance?

1 Corinthians 6:12–20

Sometimes, sexual desire is viewed like any other appetite— like a good meal. This passage blows that argument apart. What does this passage say about the body and sex?

1 Corinthians 7:1–9

Imagine a first-century woman who historically had no rights at all being given the "right" to her own sexual desire for her husband! What new insights does this passage give you about sex and marriage?

1 Thessalonians 4: 1–8
Why do you think God puts such stringent boundaries here around the sexual experience?

Romans 1: 18–32
What does it mean to exchange your glory as a man or woman created in his image for something "lesser than"? What does this passage teach about homosexuality?

The Bride of Christ

Purity of body and soul is about being made the bride of Christ. It's the reason why it all matters, in the ultimate sense.

Revelation 21:1–7
What motivates you in this passage to want to live like a woman who belongs to God?

Acknowledgments

This book is not one I dreamed of writing. None of my wistful lists of lifetime goals include an entry of authoring a book about sex. Somehow I stumbled into writing this book — ironically, with more fervor and passion than anything I have ever written. Literally compelled to write about women and sexuality, I was gripped by the subject from start to finish. It was as though I'd been carried out to sea on a huge wave and kept there for months, rowing and rowing.

I should first thank Dr. Paul and Shirley Simms of Purdue University for an invitation to speak at a large college gathering there that awakened in me the desire to explore the sexual scene as so many young women find it these days. During this time, my daughter, Allison, a great joy in my life, was finishing her undergraduate work at the University of North Carolina at Chapel Hill, where she had joined my old college sorority. From the stories she brought home, I was initially startled at how much had changed in twenty-five years. The hook-up scene, the casualness with which men and women serviced each other sexually, the waning of romance and of the pleasure of being pursued by a man for something other than sex — these struck deep notes of grief in me that eventually translated into study and prayer and finally writing.

I cannot begin to thank the women who have shared their

stories with me in the context of a private counseling practice here in Raleigh and those who have poured out their tales after I've spoken in seminars and conferences elsewhere. I am grateful for your honesty and for the privilege of having a small part in the reclamation of your hearts. Please know that I've tried to preserve the integrity of your stories while disguising the source.

Many people have had a hand in bringing this book to completion. To Linda Glasford, Greg Johnson, and Sandra Vander Zicht, my special thanks for believing in this book from the start. To the marketing team at Zondervan so willing to brainstorm the title and the packaging of an idea into an attractive form, I am grateful. My thanks to Leanne Payne and the Pastoral Care Ministries Team for opening up my understanding of the freedom of repentance and the life the gospel is meant to bring us. I am grateful to Myra Hodges and many others for their peek into the past. Connally Gillam has supplied great stories and much insight; I am truly in her debt. Sally Breedlove has been my own personal Bible consultant, always available with a fresh idea solidly rooted in truth. And finally, this book would not exist in this form without the faithfulness of a small team of people who have prayed regularly for this effort and for the women who will read it. My deep gratitude to Jennifer Ennis, Edith Struick, Dianne Gorsuch, Carol Taylor, Jan Shacklett, Ruth Brooks, and Clyde and MaryLynne Hodson, as well as a host of women scattered hither and yon who are concerned for the relational world a generation of young women are inheriting from us. May God reward you truly.

Notes

Preface

1. John 8:34–36 TNIV.

Chapter 1: Longing for Love

1. Danielle Crittenden, *What Our Mothers Didn't Tell Us: Why Happiness Eludes the Modern Woman* (New York: Simon & Schuster, 1999), 39.

Chapter 2: What Women Lose

1. Jay Dixit, "Heartbreak and Home Runs: The Power of First Experiences," *Psychology Today* (January 2010), 62.
2. Louann Brizendine, *The Female Brain* (New York: Broadway, 2006).
3. Barbara Defoe Whitehead, *Why There Are No Good Men Left* (New York: Broadway, 2003), 31.
4. Danielle Crittenden, *What Our Mothers Didn't Tell Us* (New York: Simon & Schuster, 1999), 31.
5. Wendy Shalit, *A Return to Modesty: Discovering the Lost Virtue* (New York: Simon & Schuster, 1999), 34.
6. Ibid.
7. Andrew Morton, *Madonna* (New York: St. Martin's Press, 2001), 21.
8. Matthew 7:13–14.
9. See Ephesians 4:19.
10. Rob Bell, *Sex God* (Grand Rapids: Zondervan, 2007), 76.
11. Quoted in Shalit, *Return to Modesty*, 88.

Chapter 3: A Woman's Power

1. Bruce Springsteen, "Secret Garden" (Sony Records, 1995).
2. Genesis 2:18.
3. John and Stasi Eldredge, *Captivating* (Nashville: Nelson, 2005), 42.
4. Genesis 1: 26–27 NLT, emphasis mine.

5. Isaiah 49:15.

6. John Eldredge, *Wild at Heart* (Nashville: Nelson, 2001), 182.

7. Mike Mason, *The Mystery of Marriage* (Sisters, Ore.: Multnomah, 1985), 111.

8. Wendy Shalit, *A Return to Modesty* (New York: Simon & Schuster, 1999), 98.

9. George Gilder, *Men and Marriage* (Baton Rouge, La: Pelican, 1985), 5.

10. Ibid., 11.

11. Ibid., 12.

12. Proverbs 6:25–29.

Chapter 4: Power and Seduction

1. Kelly Cohen, *Loose Girl* (New York: Hyperion, 2008), 98. (emphasis mine)

2. Ibid., 165.

3. Proverbs 7:21–23 NASB.

4. See Philip Yancey's wonderful book *The Jesus I Never Knew* (Grand Rapids: Zondervan, 1995), 74–78, 267–69.

5. Actually this someone was the Danish philosopher and theologian Søren Kierkegaard.

6. John 1:14 NASB.

7. Rob Bell, *Sex God* (Grand Rapids: Zondervan, 2007), 98.

8. Ibid., 123.

9. This story is found in another book I've written (*What's He Really Thinking? How to Be a Relational Genius with the Man in Your Life* [Nashville: Nelson, 2008]).

Chapter 5: Protective Fences

1. Diane E. Levin and Jean Kilbourne, *So Sexy, So Soon* (New York: Random House, 2009), 35.

2. Deuteronomy 24:5.

3. Naomi Wolf, *Promiscuities* (New York: Random House, 1997), 119–36.

4. Patricia Weitz, *College Girl* (New York: Riverhead, New York, 2008), 184.

Chapter 6: Stepping on Each Other's Toes

1. Ephesians 5:27.

2. Proverbs 30:18–19, emphasis mine.

3. Laura Sessions Stepp, *Unhooked: How Young Women Pursue Sex, Delay Love and Lose at Both* (New York: Riverhead, 2007), 72.

4. Danielle Crittenden, *What Our Mothers Didn't Tell Us* (New York: Simon & Schuster, 1999), 36.

5. Wendy Shalit, *A Return to Modesty* (New York: Simon & Schuster, 1999), 147.

6. John 8:1–11.

7. John 8:7 TNIV.

8. John 8:10–11.

9. Frederick Buechner, *Whistling in the Dark* (San Francisco: Harper SanFrancisco, 1993), 78–79.

10. Lisa Bevere, *Kissed the Girls and Made Them Cry* (Nashville: Nelson, 2002), 77.

Chapter 7: What Really Happens in Sex

1. John Eldredge, *The Journey of Desire* (Nashville: Nelson, 2000), 126.

2. Genesis 2:24 NASB.

3. Song of Songs 5:1–2.

4. Barbara Wilson, *Kiss Me Again* (Sisters, Ore.: Multnomah, 2009), 149.

5. Genesis 24:66–67.

6. This is why you read some of the strongest words in the Bible: "Marriage should be honored by all, and the marriage bed kept pure, for God will judge the adulterer and all the sexually immoral" (Hebrews 13:4).

7. Lauren Winner, *Real Sex* (Grand Rapids: Brazos, 2005), 38.

8. Heard in a television interview with Harrison's sister days after his death.

9. Heard in a presentation by Leanne Payne, Pastoral Care Ministries.

10. 1 Corinthians 6:18 TNIV.

11. 1 Corinthians 6:19 TNIV.

12. Mike Mason, *The Mystery of Marriage* (Sisters, Ore: Multnomah, 1985), 122.

13. Zephaniah 3:17 NASB.

14. Eldredge, *Journey of Desire*, 128.

15. Ephesians 5:31–32.

16. John Donne, "Holy Sonnet XIX," in *Masterpieces of Religious Verse*, ed. James Dalton Morrison (Grand Rapids: Baker, 1977), 102.

17. Pamela Rowen-Herzog, "Dialogue," Circle of Hope Church, Philadelphia, Pennsylvania (2001). Used by permission.

Chapter 8: Getting Back Your Heart

1. Lisa Bevere, *Kissed the Girls and Made Them Cry* (Nashville: Nelson, 2002), 122.

2. This phrase seems to have been coined by Mike Long, a public school educator. See his book *Parents: Everyone Is Not Doing It* (Ottawa, Ill.: Jameson, 2000).

3. Ephesians 1:18–19, emphasis mine.

4. For insightful help, see Elmer Towns, *Fasting for Spiritual Breakthrough* (Ventura, Calif.: Regal, 1990).

5. Isaiah 58:6.

6. Hebrews 4:15–16.

7. Galatians 3:13–14.

8. Isaiah 30:18, emphasis mine.

9. John 8:31.

10. See Barbara Wilson, *Kiss Me Again* (Sisters, Ore: Multnomah, 2009).

11. James 5:16.

12. Malachi 4:2.

13. Hosea 2:14–15.

14. Genesis 28–30.

15. Genesis 29:20.

16. Genesis 29:32.

17. I am indebted to Tim Keller of Redeemer Presbyterian Church in New York City for this startling parallel.

Chapter 9: Recognizing a Good Man

1. Isaiah 48:17.

2. Psalm 27:10 NASB.

3. Robin Norwood, *Women Who Love Too Much* (New York: Pocket, 1986), 40.

4. John 13:23.

Chapter 10: Giving Yourself Away

1. Song of Songs 3:5.

2. For an excellent discussion, see Lisa Bevere, *Kissed the Girls and Made Them Cry* (Nashville: Nelson, 2002).

3. Bevere, *Kissed the Girls and Made Them Cry*, 129.

4. 1 Timothy 1:22.

5. Told by Connally Gillam. Used by permission.

6. Ronald Rolheiser, *The Holy Longing* (New York: Doubleday, 1999), 193.

7. Ibid., 192.

Chapter 11: The Good Relationship

1. Proverbs 31:3.

2. Proverbs 31:4 – 5.

3. Proverbs 31:8 – 9.

4. Frederick Buechner, *A Room to Remember* (San Francisco: Harper SanFrancisco, 1984), 68 – 69.

Chapter 12: The Making of a Man

1. Proverbs 28:1.

2. Norman Mailer, *Cannibals and Christians* (New York: Dial, 1966), 201. The concept is further explored in Frank Pittman's insightful book *Man Enough* (New York: Perigee, 1993).

3. John Eldredge, *Wild at Heart* (Nashville: Nelson, 2001), 16.

4. Robert Bly, *Iron John* (Reading, Mass.: Addison-Wesley, 1990), 135.

5. Ibid., 136.

6. Eldredge, *Wild at Heart*, 91.

7. Ibid., 115.

8. Cited in "Why Men Won't Commit," in Barbara Dafoe Whitehead and David Popenoe, "The State of Our Unions: The Social Health of Marriage in America" (a 2002 study commissioned by The National Marriage Project).

9. 1 Thessalonians 4:3 – 5 NASB.

10. 1 Corinthians 7:5.

11. Ephesians 5:25.

12. 1 Peter 3:7.

13. Job 38:2 – 4.

Afterword

1. Psalm 90:17 NKJV.

About the Author

*P*aula Rinehart is an author and counselor whose great pleasure is helping women understand the deeper issues of their hearts in the light of God's love and truth.

She is the author of the widely acclaimed book *Strong Women, Soft Hearts* and the award-winning bestseller *Choices,* which she wrote with her husband. Her most recent book is *What's He Really Thinking? How to Be a Relationship Genius with the Man in Your Life.* Her articles have appeared in *Christianity Today, Marriage Partnership,* and *Discipleship Journal.* Paula and her husband ministered for many years on staff with The Navigators with college students and career singles. They live in Raleigh, North Carolina, where Paula maintains a private counseling practice. She also speaks to college groups and women's groups around the country on the topics of sexuality, relationships, and intimacy with God.

For information about scheduling Paula for women's conferences, seminars, and retreats, email Single Source Speakers (Tom@singlesourcespeakers.com) or call 615-263-4148. To contact Paula, email her at paularinehart@mentorlink.org or paulacrinehart@gmail.com. For more information, visit www.PaulaRinehart.com.

Share Your Thoughts

With the Author: Your comments will be forwarded to the author when you send them to *zauthor@zondervan.com*.

With Zondervan: Submit your review of this book by writing to *zreview@zondervan.com*.

Free Online Resources at
www.zondervan.com

Zondervan AuthorTracker: Be notified whenever your favorite authors publish new books, go on tour, or post an update about what's happening in their lives at www.zondervan.com/authortracker.

Daily Bible Verses and Devotions: Enrich your life with daily Bible verses or devotions that help you start every morning focused on God. Visit www.zondervan.com/newsletters.

Free Email Publications: Sign up for newsletters on Christian living, academic resources, church ministry, fiction, children's resources, and more. Visit www.zondervan.com/newsletters.

Zondervan Bible Search: Find and compare Bible passages in a variety of translations at www.zondervanbiblesearch.com.

Other Benefits: Register yourself to receive online benefits like coupons and special offers, or to participate in research.

Z ZONDERVAN®

ZONDERVAN.com/
AUTHORTRACKER
follow your favorite authors